"DANGER LIKE...

The tragic history o... ...
legends of sea monst... ...ships, demons and waterspouts.

JANUARY 21, 1921. The Japanese freighter **Raifuku Maru** voyages from the icy waters of her homeland to the blue seas of the tropical Atlantic. As the ship steams past the Bahamas into the dread waters of the "Devil's Triangle," she sends a radio message imploring for help . . . then silence.

WHAT DID THE WORD "DAGGER" MEAN? Some speculate the ship had fallen prey to a giant waterspout, more than a mile high with a shaft fifteen hundred feet across. All we know for certain is that after her distress call nothing more was ever heard from the **Raifuku Maru**, another victim of . . .

THE DEVIL'S TRIANGLE

THE DEVIL'S TRIANGLE

RICHARD WINER

BANTAM BOOKS
TORONTO · NEW YORK · LONDON

RLI: VLM 10 (VLR 8–11)
      IL 10–adult

THE DEVIL'S TRIANGLE
A Bantam Book / published September 1974
2nd printing
3rd printing
4th printing
5th printing
6th printing
7th printing
8th printing

Published simultaneously in the United States and Canada

Bantam Books are published by Bantam Books, Inc. Its trade-
mark, consisting of the words "Bantam Books" and the por-
trayal of a bantam, is registered in the United States Patent
Office and in other countries. Marca Registrada. Bantam
Books, Inc., 666 Fifth Avenue, New York, New York 10019.

PRINTED IN THE UNITED STATES OF AMERICA

THIS BOOK IS DEDICATED TO
THE NEXT VICTIM(S)

Contents

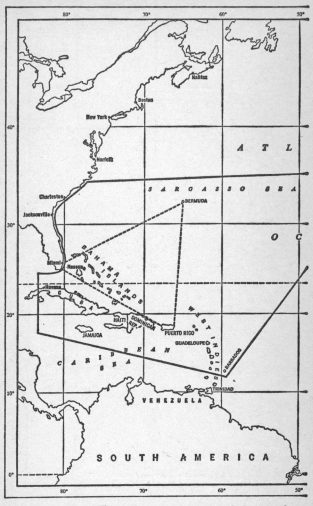

The outlined area is the actual sector of the North
Atlantic in which the mysterious disappearances have
occurred. The dotted line section is the area usually

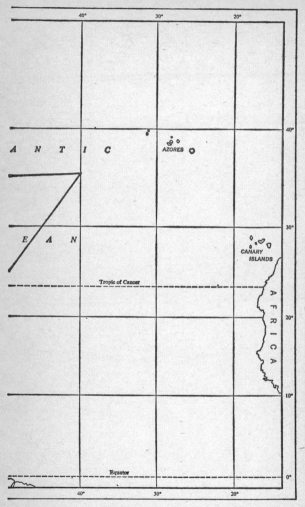

referred to as the "Devil's" or "Bermuda Triangle."
However, it is only one quarter of the true triangle
or trapezium.

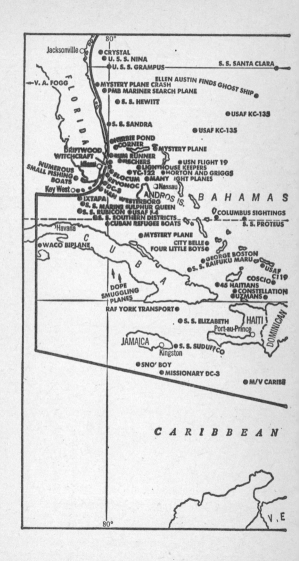

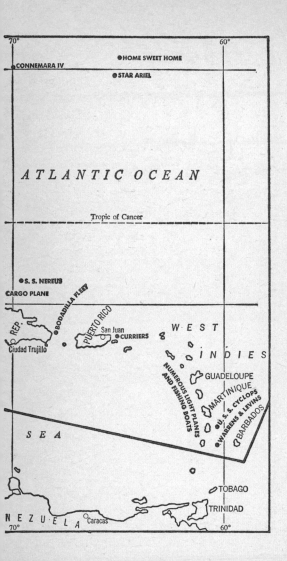

70°   60°

●HOME SWEET HOME

● CONNEMARA IV

● STAR ARIEL

ATLANTIC OCEAN

Tropic of Cancer

● S. S. NEREUS
CARGO PLANE

● BODADILLA FLEET

REP.

● PUERTO RICO

San Juan

Ciudad Trujillo   ● CURRIERS

W E S T

I N D I E S

NUMEROUS LIGHT PLANES
AND FISHING BOATS

GUADELOUPE

MARTINIQUE

●U. S. S. CYCLOPS

●WARRENS & LEVINS

BARBADOS

S E A

TOBAGO

TRINIDAD

N E Z U E L A ○ Caracas

70°   60°

Introduction

Just across the harbor from Hong Kong in Kowloon there was a flagrant waterfront establishment known as Mike's Bar. Mike was a full-blooded Chinaman. His clientele consisted of sailors, members of the crown colony's underworld, waterfront bums, prostitutes, characters in general, and even an occasional lost or misguided tourist. The saloon's claim to fame was that it was the roughest bar in the world. Even the notorious Quinn's Bar in Tahiti couldn't rival Mike's Place. When Mike's patrons were not actively engaged in a brawl, they were probably watching one. On those rare occasions when peace and tranquility prevailed, the main occupation of Mike's patrons was swapping stories—usually sea stories. And it was here in 1967, the same year that an unhappy customer did Mike in with a broken bottle, that I first heard of a small mysterious section of the sea halfway around the world called "The Devil's Triangle." It was described as a place where ships sail off the end of the earth, where planes climb up into the sky never to come down again, and where sailors and airmen disappear forever.

Actually, "The Devil's Triangle" is not a triangle at all. It is a trapezium, a four-sided area in which no two sides or angles are the same. And the first four letters of the word *trapezium* more than adequately describe it.

Having lived in Florida for over fifteen years, I had,

from time to time, read newspaper stories telling of some ship, plane, or yacht simply vanishing without a trace. But the magnitude of these happenings never occurred to me until that day in Mike's Bar.

San Salvador Island in the Bahamas, where Christopher Columbus supposedly made his first landfall in the New World, is located well inside the perimeter of "The Devil's Triangle" as are Crooked Island and Rum Cay, which some historians claim was Columbus's first sighting of land. It is mentioned in the great explorer's chronicle that the night before the history-changing discovery, he and his crew saw what appeared to be a greenish glowing light that at times would move about. Anthropologists theorize that what Columbus saw were cooking fires in fishing canoes of Carib Indians moving up and down in the waves. Some oceanographers think that the greenish lights were fires on the beach and that the breaking surf distorted the color and shape of the blazes and created an illusion of movement. The philosophy of the UFOologists needs no explanation. But no matter what it was, Indians, illusions, or UFOs, that the mariners saw on that night in 1492 along the eastern fringe of the Bahama Islands, strange and unusual things have been happening in that area ever since.

Between the time you read these words and finish this book, you can be sure that this mysterious section of the Atlantic Ocean will have claimed another victim. He might be anyone from an obscure Bahamian fisherman to a prominent citizen who took off in an airplane never to be heard from again. But whomever the victim may be, it will happen. One would not have to be a prophet to predict that some of you who are now reading these words will journey out into that sea of dead ships, missing planes, doomed men, and lost hopes . . . and disappear forever.

1. Flight to Oblivion

December 5, 1945, was a typical south Florida winter day—variable winds, a chilly morning, and a balmy afternoon with clear skies. Fort Lauderdale Naval Air Station, now Hollywood–Fort Lauderdale International Airport, was a bustle of activity. World War II had been over nearly four months. In addition to the permanently based ship's company and those assigned to the base for TBM (Torpedo Bomber Medium) School, there was a large complement of navy and marine personnel awaiting discharge.

The headlines in the Miami *Herald* that day read, "CIO Splits With Truman." The weatherman had forecast a temperature drop to 38 degrees for the following morning. Three marine gunnery students at the base—Sergeant Robert Gallivan of Northamptom, Massachusetts; Private First Class Robert Gruebel of Long Island City, New York; and Corporal Allen Kosnar of Kenosha, Wisconsin—could not have cared less about politics or tomorrow's weather as they returned to their barracks from the mess hall after lunch. The subject of their conversation was being home for

Christmas and whether to attend the first or second show at the base theater that night. The picture was *What Next, Corporal Hargrave?* starring Robert Walker—a movie that they would never see.

All three were scheduled to participate in a training flight that afternoon with a squadron of five navy TBMs, also known as Avengers. Having over an hour before they were to report to the flight line, the three marines decided to "sack out" in their bunks for a while.

When it came time to leave the barracks for the operations building and a preflight briefing, Corporal Kosnar had a strange premonition not to go on the flight. To get himself excused was no problem because he had already completed his required flight time for that month. Bob Gallivan and Bob Gruebel along with twelve other marine and navy fliers reported to the operations center.

The mission of the day for Flight 19, as the squadron was designated, was a routine navigation exercise. Little did any of the six navy and eight marine airmen realize that their operation was to climax in what the navy would later refer to as one of the "strangest unsolved mysteries of the sea."

Twenty-four years later, Allen Kosnar returned to Fort Lauderdale airport to participate in a documentary film about strange unsolved mysteries of the sea. As he was exploring the old navy buildings, now used as a junior high school, he pointed to one as looking familiar. The boys' physical education locker room was the old barracks in which he was billeted along with Gallivan, Gruebel, and most of the other enlisted men of Flight 19. As Kosnar walked past the row of lockers and benches, he was silent—in deep thought. The windows being painted over rendered the building darker than normal inside. When he walked out into the sunlight, he squinted and muttered, "For some strange reason that I can't explain, I decided not to go on the flight that day."

For Sergeant Gallivan, a veteran aerial gunner with three years of Pacific combat duty, this was to be just another routine flight. To Private First Class Gruebel with less than a year in the service, this was another wonderful opportunity to fly. His buddies nicknamed him "Yo Yo" because of his eagerness to fly whenever he could. His goal in life, however, was to enter the priesthood after his enlistment expired. He had just written home that he would see his family at Christmas mass in a few short weeks.

Flight 19 was under the command of Lieutenant Charles C. Taylor of Corpus Christi, Texas, a six-year navy veteran. Flying with him in the lead plane were Aviation Radioman Third Class Walter Parpart and Aviation Ordnanceman Third Class George Devlin. The two enlisted men were from the same Brooklyn neighborhood. The other pilots and their crews were Ensign Joseph Bossi of Arkansas City, Kansas; Seaman First Class Herman Thelander of Kimbrew, Minnesota; and Seaman First Class Bert Valuk of Bloomfield, New Jersey; Marine Lieutenant Forest Gerber of New Ulm, Minnesota, and Private First Class William Lightfoot of Lexington, Illinois (Kosnar was to have flown as gunner in this plane); Marine Captain George W. Stivers of Piedmont, Missouri (Gruebel and Gallivan flew in this plane); and Marine Captain Edward Powers of Mount Vernon, New York; Staff Sergeant Howell Thompson of Chicago, Illinois; and Staff Sergeant George Paonessa of Mamaroneck, New York.

It was 1:30 P.M. when the five pilots and their crews reported to the flight line for a preflight check of their respective planes. The Avenger was one of the largest and most powerful single-engine propeller planes ever built. It was used from both aircraft carriers and island bases. The wings could be folded back for carrier use. It had a wing span of over fifty-two feet and was powered by a sixteen-hundred-horsepower Wright Cyclone engine. The plane was able to attain an air speed of nearly three-hundred miles per hour and could carry either a torpedo or two thousand pounds of bombs. The plane's crew of three consisted of a pilot, a radioman, and a gunner. TBMs were responsible for some of the most decisive American naval air victories in the Pacific during World War II. Most spectacular was the sinking of the world's largest battleship, the *Yamato*, along with her escort consisting of the cruiser *Yahagi* and four destroyers. All six Japanese ships went to the bottom in less than an hour after the first Avenger spotted them.

Flight 19's preflight weather check showed surface winds of twenty knots with gusts to thirty and scattered clouds. Although these conditions would have been rough for small boats, it was the kind of weather TBMs were built to fly in.

At 2 P.M., Lieutenant Taylor's plane was airborne, and ten minutes later, the five planes with their fourteen men were in formation and winging east over the Atlantic toward the wreck of a target ship just south of Bimini in the Bahamas. After making their mock torpedo runs at the concrete hulk, Flight 19 regrouped and commenced with the day's mission—a routine navigation training flight that was scheduled to take them due east for 160 miles, north for 40 miles, and then west south west back to their base, a triangular course that fit well into the Bermuda or "Devil's Triangle."

At 3:45, fifteen minutes before the flight was due to land, Corporal Kosnar was in the barrack's day-room sealing a letter he had just written to his parents. One hundred and fifty miles up the Florida coast at Banana River Naval Air Station, now Patrick Air Force Base serving Cape Canaveral, Lieutenant Harry G. Cone of Gainesville, Florida, and his crew of twelve men had just reported to the operations room. Under routine procedure, they were to stand by as the "ready crew" should any of the huge Martin Mariner PBM flying boats based there be needed for a search and rescue mission. The tower operators at Fort Lauderdale Naval Air Station were waiting to be relieved at 4 P.M. As the tower's chief radioman checked over his log before turning the watch over to his relief, the tower received a frantic message from Lieutenant Taylor: "Calling tower, this is an emergency. We seem to be off course. We cannot see land . . . repeat . . . we cannot see land."

"What is your position?" the tower radioed back.

"We are not sure of our position," radioed Lieutenant Taylor. "We can't be sure just where we are. We seem to be lost."

The tower operators were startled. How could five planes with experienced crews be lost with fair to good flight conditions? "Assume bearing due west," the tower radioed.

Taylor replied, "We don't know which way is west. Everything is wrong . . . strange. We can't be sure of any direction. Even the ocean doesn't look as it should!"

Just after 4 P.M. the flight leader suddenly turned the command over to Captain Stivers with whom Gallivan and Gruebel were flying. By this time word of Flight 19's predicament had spread around the base.

Kosnar rushed over to the tower and at 4:25 P.M. heard Captain Stivers's voice, "We are not sure where we are. We think we must be 225 miles northeast of base." After a few seconds of static, the same voice came in again: "It looks like we are entering white water." A broken voice then came in: "We're completely lost." Then silence.

By this time, Lieutenant Cone in his Mariner flying boat was already heading out over the Atlantic from Banana River toward the last estimated position of Flight 19. The Mariner with its 124-foot wing span was bigger than a flying fortress. Her crew of thirteen was well oriented in search and rescue operations. The giant plane carried every conceivable type of rescue apparatus from self-inflating life rafts to waterproofed radio transmitters that upon contact with water would transmit a distress call for hours. The plane carried enough fuel to remain aloft for over twenty-four hours.

Less than a half hour later, the Mariner's radio operator, Aviation Radioman Third Class J. Jorden of Oakland, California, sent a message to the base that they were nearing the last assumed position of the five lost Avengers but could see nothing. Others in the Mariner's crew included Lieutenant J. G. W. G. Jeffrey of Los Angeles, California; Ensign R. M. Allen of Sumter, South Carolina; Ensign G. D. Arceneaux of Lafayette, Indiana; Ensign L. A. Eliason of Montevideo, Minnesota; Aviation Ordnanceman Third Class J. Mendez of Jacksonville, Florida; Aviation Machinist Mate First Class D. E. Peterson of Carpenter, Arkansas; Seaman First Class W. D. Cargill of Columbus, Alabama; Aviation Radioman Third Class R. C. Cameron of Hondo, Texas; Seaman First Class P. B. Newman of North Ill, Pennsylvania; Aviation Ordnanceman Third Class J. F. Osterheld of Salinas, California; and Seaman First Class Joseph Zywicki of Chicago, Illinois.

The Mariner sent in one more position report. Then the number *thirteen* proved unlucky for Harry Cone and his crew of twelve aboard the big PBM, for the giant plane was never heard from again.

At 7:04 P.M., the tower at Opa Locka Naval Air Station in Miami heard a very faint message, "FT—FT." These were part of Flight 19's call letters. Could one of the Avengers still have been aloft almost two hours after the last plane in the squadron should have run out of fuel? No other plane would have used those letters.

Navy and coast guard vessels had put to sea immediately after contact with the Mariner was lost. By dawn the next day, 242 aircraft and 18 surface vessels engaged in the search were joined by the carrier *Solomons* and her complement of 35 planes. The operation became the most intensive air-sea search ever conducted. As the day progressed more ships and planes joined the search that covered over 280,000 square miles. Even the Everglades and the Gulf of Mexico were searched. Land parties scoured hundreds of miles of Florida and Bahamian shorelines.

On Monday, December 9, an air force plane reported sighting two life rafts three hundred miles northeast of Miami. A coast guard cutter dispatched to the scene reported them to be only packing cases. As darkness fell on December 10, the search was called off.

The Navy Department was in a quandary. How could six planes and twenty-seven men disappear in a relatively small area of the Atlantic Ocean? Later after a Naval Board of Inquiry, in which Lieutenant Taylor was posthumously absolved of any blame, one of the board members concluded, "We're not even able to make a good guess as to what happened." "They vanished as completely as if they'd flown to

Mars," said another officer. A coast guard spokesman said, "We don't know what the hell is going on out there."

Many theories ranging from UFOs to a massive midair collision have been conjectured, but nothing conclusive was ever proven. If there had been a massive collision involving all five Avengers, surely some debris and flotsam would have been found. Five planes could not simultaneously exhaust their fuel supplies. When the first one went down, one of the others would have radioed the fact and so on until the last plane went down. There have been many instances of Avengers being forced down at sea and remaining afloat as long as thirty minutes. All of the planes in Flight 19 carried self-inflating life rafts and other survival gear.

Richard Adams, now a Fort Lauderdale realtor, piloted one of the Mariner rescue planes out of Banana River NAS during the search. He recalled that a cold front passed through the area on that day bringing about an abrupt change in wind direction, a change that could have caused the flight, which was compensating for twenty- to thirty-knot southeasterly winds, to have been driven several hundred miles south of its estimated position by the forty-knot northwesterly winds. But, had this been the case, the planes would have been someplace close to Andros Island or the Exumas in the Bahamas. And from the time of their first indication of trouble until their last message, the crews surely would have spotted one of the many islands beneath them. As for the missing Mariner, Adams suggested that the Mariners were often referred to as "flying gas tanks" because of the huge fuel tanks built into their hulls. He mentioned that it was customary for the pilot or copilot to search the crew members before each flight for matches or cigarette lighters due to the danger from fire. Adams speculated that Cone and his crew took off in such a hurry that this precaution was overlooked, and one of the crew may have attempted to light a cigarette.

A merchant vessel, the S.S. *Gaines Mills*, reported seeing and hearing a loud explosion off Melbourne Beach at 7:30 that night. But that would have been two hours after the Mariner's last message. The huge flying boat certainly would not have kept radio silence that long during a search and rescue mission. And if one radio went out, the Mariner carried a standby set completely independent of the first one. If both did, by chance, go out, the plane would have returned to base immediately. No wreckage of the Mariner, as would have been evidence of an explosion, was ever found.

Manson Valentine, Ph.D., a world-renowned explorer, specializing in Mayan and Aztec cultures, who is presently investigating what might be the ruins of a sunken city off the Bahamas, expressed a completely different theory: "They are still here, but in a different dimension as a result of a magnetic phenomenon that could have been set up by a UFO."

Henry White, an oceanographer with Nova University, suggested that the mention of "white water" in the last few seconds of communication with the five Avengers could mean a huge violent squall, sometimes referred to as a "white squall," with winds so rampant that the tempest-driven rain blended completely with the wind-churned ocean to create a phenomenon so fierce that it could easily disintegrate five planes. But again there was no debris or bodies found. And the five planes were completely disoriented and in panic situation 30 minutes before the mention of "white water."

Commander Robert Cox, USN, Ret., was senior

flight instructor at the Naval Air Station in Fort Lauderdale when Flight 19 vanished. In fact, he was leading another squadron at the time and actually talking plane to plane with Lieutenant Taylor. A letter dated December 5, 1970, and written by Cox states:

It is odd that I write this letter 25 years to the day that the events of the mystery occurred as I have refrained from doing so in the past when this story came to life. The supposed events do make good copy and without much trouble can become a modern saga. As a matter of fact, I was the one person who was in constant radio contact with Lt. Taylor after he became disoriented. I was up with a formation flight of 12 planes and talked with Lt. Taylor until a relay burned out in my transmitter and I landed for repairs or to get another plane and lead his ill-fated flight back to land. I knew exactly where he was and made every attempt to tell him. There was a rather lengthy investigation at the time and I was a principal witness.

Frankly there is no mystery at all, I assure you. A chain of unfortunate events and plain human frailty caused the loss of life in the TBMs, and the PBM-3 [Mariner] most likely would have exploded on any flight it took . . . this one had nothing to do with the mishap.

Commander Cox, like Corporal Kosnar, was a first-hand witness to the occurrence. His theories result from direct participation. They are directly opposed to those of Dr. Valentine. But hundreds of "factual" books have been written about UFOs, and thousands of "authentic" sightings have been reported. I, myself, a writer, reporter, and photographer, have never seen anything strange or even close to "occult" during many flights over and voyages into the "triangle." I cannot but feel skeptical for this reason. Yet, as I think about the known facts, I also wonder if there is something unusual happening in the "Devil's Triangle."

Valentine, White, and Adams expressed nothing more than conjectures. Commander Cox, who was as close to the situation as anyone, also presented a conjecture. Are the mysteries of the "Devil's Triangle" nothing more than a chain of logically explainable events? There are many pros and cons. But the United States Navy has never officially closed the case by resolving what fate befell Flight 19.

Down through the years there have been an untold number of theories about what might have happened to Flight 19 and the PBM Mariner. But there were three men in contact with Flight 19 during the entire ordeal. The men, Radioman Second Class Melvin Baker, Radioman Third Class George Rowic, and Seaman First Class Gene Dionne, were based at an army-navy communications exchange headquarters at Port Everglades, which was less than a mile from Fort Lauderdale Naval Air Station. The purpose of this base was to handle every type of communication from official personnel transfer orders to assuming control of search and rescue operations from Banana River Naval Air Station southward around the Florida Keys and into the Gulf of Mexico. It was also charged with movement of vessels within a range of four hundred miles seaward and maintained the ships' positions with colored pins on a huge wall map. Seven of the base's thirteen receivers had the capacity to reach throughout the world. The men stationed there maintained twenty-four-hour watch on several frequencies with special emphasis on 3000, the national distress frequency.

Melvin Baker wrote in a letter dated May 23, 1973:

At our station, every minute of every day a log was kept of all communications on a single roll. This was continuous roll paper about like a paper towel roll. This fiasco from start to "search abandoned negative" was one full roll and part of another. Every message, several a minute, was recorded and identified. This was the only complete record of all transmissions. When it became apparent that a serious investigation would ensue, an officer from the admiral's office at Naval District Headquarters in Miami came to our station to get this log. I refused to give it to him with the backing of my operations officer, Lt. Thompson. The log was locked in our safe until the first day of the hearings by Secretary of the Navy Forrestal, and at that time the log was placed in Mr. Thompson's hands for his presentation. We knew of nothing final in this investigation, but rumors were that a vice-admiral and some of his underlings as well as the Fort Lauderdale Naval Air Station operations officer were "busted" to some extent. We of the communications were never questioned nor were we contacted in any manner. We were all enlisted men, you see, and only the log was introduced into court, and we never knew to what extent. It was never returned, which was against regulations. I just hope they "got" the right people, but I am sure they did not receive their due.

On that fatal December day when Baker, Rowic, and Dionne were manning the communications center, seven voice receivers were going full blast all of the time with planes, ships, boats, and other stations constantly talking. However, the men on duty were used to this and found no difficulty in following the trends of the many radio conversations. They were cognizant from the beginning of the stress among Flight 19. However, the Naval Air Station's operations officer originally directed the flight; thus, the three radiomen just listened.

Baker wrote:

I knew when the voice of the leader [Taylor] took on the quality of fright and dismay, so I immediately cut in and asked for his confirming that he was lost, which he did.

He described the situation as their having run into an eighty mile per hour head wind and lost direction. The very first step was to have a call made to Naval Air Station Ft. Lauderdale radio communications. This was by telephone. We requested the exact training flight pattern, time of departure, amount of fuel in the planes, exact expired flight time, and ratio of fuel use of the particular planes. While this was being done, I continued my conversation with the flight leader . . . and I might say now . . . his NAS [Naval Air Station] control never came on the air with another message to him . . . not one . . . not even a peep. The flight leader had decided he had been blown over the Gulf of Mexico.

Baker immediately had a map and weather check made and found that no such winds existed over land or the Gulf of Mexico. However it was discovered that high winds were prevailing over the Atlantic where Flight 19 was supposed to be. Concluding that the five planes were unmistakably lost, Baker called Miami Naval Headquarters requesting a radio direction finder fix on the planes. A radio direction finder is basically a powerful receiver that can home in on the source of a radio transmission and give the direction from whence it is originating. Two of these devices at different locations can range in on a signal source, and ascertain the position of the transmitting radio.

Baker kept Taylor talking in order that Miami could zero in on the direction of the flight. But that would only give one bearing. Two were needed to pinpoint the flight's location. As time passed, Miami Naval Headquarters was requested every few minutes to give a radio directional fix. Each time it gave the same reply, "We are trying." By now Lieutenant Hatch, the communications officer, as well as Radioman Ted Ardary and many of the off-duty operators were in the communications room.

Baker continued:

I tuned down the power on my transmitter to a point I knew the flight leader could just still hear me and I was able to determine that he was not over the Gulf. I had the flight leader switch radio frequencies to the local working distress channel, but do not remember if we had given word to change to the trainees. This was not usually done so long as communications were workable. This isolated myself and the flight leader [Taylor] on this frequency. His home base knew this and could listen which I know they did. We could, of course, still have communications with the other planes, but they seldom got on the air. I let all concerned know what I had done with the power drop and tried to make them all know that I was positive. Too, we had alerted every known vessel in the area for four hundred miles. Lt. Thompson had all of the rescue vessels in the harbor fueled and standing by at the edge of the Gulf Stream ready for any duty. All air bases in Florida were alerted to have their planes stand by. From our calculations, gas was getting low. Repeatedly we got negative results from Headquarters Miami on the radio fix. The men on the flight began to get frantic. One came on the air while I had the power down and said he refused to stay in formation and fly with the others as he felt they were heading out to sea. I tried to convince him to stay, but after a while he left the flight and was never heard from again.

Ironically, several months before all of this happened, a patrol vessel was brought into Port Everglades for decommissioning. The men from the communication center managed to "appropriate" some of the electronic gear from the vessel. From this they managed to put together their own radio direction finder. It was accurate to within a fraction of a degree in any direction, and they had its operation so refined that they could obtain a fix on a radio signal within ninety seconds. However, an officer from the admiral's office at Miami Headquarters heard about this home-made "Rube Goldberg" device that was more efficient than those costing the navy thousands of dollars. Orders were given for it to be destroyed.

Again Miami Naval Headquarters was asked about the RDF (radio direction finder) fix. This request was made by phone to the office of the admiral in charge. And again the reply was, "We are still trying."

Baker continued:

Now with something less than an hour's fuel the flight leader sighted land. He described the mass in detail from the air, and I was one hundred per cent convinced that he was over Andros Island [in the Bahamas] south and east of his base. I had the map checked and rechecked by his description and know to this day that he was over Andros. I gave him a bearing to fly that I knew headed him toward us. We had a line-of-sight transmitter, five feet tall and three feet wide and of the finest caliber made. The use of the instrument—line of sight uninhibited transmission as clear as a telephone. Line of sight on the sea is fifty miles . . . allow the best of working conditions and a plane over the sea and not a cloud in the sky, and I would say this transmitter could not possibly surpass seventy-five miles . . . never at all. I talked to the flight leader on this transmitter for four continuous minutes, gradually cutting down the power. He could still hear me, but I think that I never convinced him that I knew what I was doing. I pleaded with his superiors at the Lauderdale NAS [Naval Air Station] to please issue him orders to fly by my signals. They would not come on the air. They did not ever come on the air. Still on reduced power, I begged the leader. I knew where he was. I figured his flight speed versus when he crossed over Andros Island, and I knew as well as others in the communications building that he was coming in, but he would not listen. He told me that if he were that close he would be able to see land. I told him not if he were flying parallel to us. I related his fuel capacity and told him he had enough left to make a fifty-mile, three-hundred-and-sixty-degree circle and couldn't miss. I couldn't convince him. He finally told me he was going to change course, which he did. I power-followed him. He got weaker and I told him so . . . again begging him to listen . . . begging his headquarters to order him, but no one would give in. The leader became more faint by the second. He couldn't hear me in a short while except at intervals. He continued on in the same direction and went to his fuel exhaustion.

While Baker was communicating with Lieutenant Taylor, the others in the communication center were busily plotting estimated positions, contacting vessels, and other planes in the area. After the final signal from Flight 19 had faded out, Miami Naval Headquarters was again contacted by Radioman Baker. He wrote:

Still no fix. I berated them, I badgered them, and still nothing. We had recalculated the flight situation from every angle and concluded no possibility of fuel remaining. No communication could be made. But we kept on forever and ever, it seemed. Now I do not remember the exact time, but from the best of my memory after two hours and forty-five minutes from my last audible conversation with the flight leader, Miami Naval Headquarters came in with a fix. We continued on and on. George Rowic and I stayed all night, all the following day, that night, and on for seventy-two straight hours . . . eating at the radios and expending waste upon the ground outside the door. Ted Ardary, Gene Dionne, a fellow named Proctor, and several others were there most of the time.

About the missing Mariner PBM flying boat, Baker wrote:

George Rowic and I were in communication with the "Dumbo" [a nickname given Mariner flying boats] from prior to take off until he was gone. As the "Dumbo" came to the fix location we had him on his transmitter at intervals ordered to be no longer than every three minutes. He reported on site and saw nothing. He was told to begin tight circles still broadcasting at the assigned intervals whether he had anything to say or not. He had not made much of a start at this circle flying when he went off the air. It was disputed among us: "Did his transmitter give out a blast sound?" Personally, I could not say but thought not. I continued to call him over and over for a long time.

As Baker was using voice communication in attempting to reestablish contact with the Mariner, a heavy cruiser was also endeavoring to contact the flying boat by means of code signals. The ship reported it was at the exact location the PBM Mariner was supposed to be at. Every available crewman aboard was sky watching. The big "Dumbo" should have been flying almost overhead. The ship had the personnel and equipment to establish its position to within one mile. It was at the spot the big flying boat was supposedly circling when contact with it was lost. The ship reported that the search plane had never been there.

From the letters and statements of those persons connected either directly or indirectly with the loss of the six aircraft, it would appear that almost all of the links are known, and all that remains is to connect them, thus solving what the navy considers one of the greatest mysteries of the sea. There are on record enough facts to draw a number of conclusions without over-conjecturing.

1. PBM Mariner flying boats were dangerous craft to fly because of the large quantity of high octane fuel carried aboard, and a number of them had exploded in midair.

2. A cold front with heavy winds had moved

through the Straits of Florida on December 5, 1945, resulting in a sudden change of wind direction from southeast to northwest.

3. Lieutenant Taylor was confused as to which direction he was from his base.

4. The fact that Radioman Baker and Lieutenant Taylor switched radio frequencies to a separate channel from the other planes could account for the tower assuming that Captain Stivers took over command of the flight. Very probably he communicated with the other planes while Taylor was occupied with Baker's efforts to guide the flight home.

5. The one plane leaving the flight and heading back in the opposite direction could lead those on the ground monitoring the radio communications to assume that panic prevailed.

6. It has been asked many times why the flight didn't follow the sun back to the west as the incident occurred not long before sunset. There could be two explanations: a cloud cover that moved in with the front; or if Taylor thought the flight was over the Gulf of Mexico, he would naturally fly away from the sun, thus heading farther out into the Atlantic Ocean.

7. Commander Cox was under the impression that he heard all of the flight leader's communications and had been talking with him until almost the end. However, Baker's radio was much more powerful and probably maintained contact with the flight somewhat longer than either Cox or Fort Lauderdale NAS. Also Baker and Taylor were on a separate channel for a portion of the time including the flight's last contact.

8. Andros Island, which is about one hundred miles or so east south east of Miami, is bordered by deep water along its eastern shoreline and miles and miles of shoals to the west of the island. It is long and narrow. These shoals extend at least fifty miles west-

ward and, from the air during inclement weather, could well confuse an aviator with the southern tip of Florida just north of the Keys. The similarities between these areas are such that Lieutenant Taylor could have assumed that he had just passed Florida and was over the Gulf. In fact, so sure was he that this had happened that he refused to heed Radioman Baker. He turned the flight around, but instead of heading back to Florida, he actually flew back toward Andros and possibly missed the island altogether. Hence, he ended up flying farther to the east . . . away from his base.

9. Andros is far enough south of where the patrol should have been that had they not compensated for the change in wind direction soon enough, they could well have been blown down into that area.

10. The planes were in all probability heading west, but bucking hurricane force winds of seventy to eighty knots, their speed over the surface would have been reduced by that much. Thus when they should have been approaching the coast of Florida, they were approaching Andros Island. It would be then that they would have been able to determine what the force of the head winds were, and once out over the water again they could have passed into an area in which the front had already passed and the winds were now diminishing.

11. Several months prior to December 5, 1945, the communications station at Port Everglades, as a result of its excellence in coordinating rescue operations, received a citation from Secretary of the Navy James Forrestal.

Assuming these facts, one can recreate the episode that spelled doom for Flight 19. Presumably shortly after 3:30 P.M. on December 5, 1945, the five Navy TBM Avengers were on the last leg of the routine training mission. Just before they were due to have sighted land, by their reckoning, they encountered a cold front containing a heavy cloud cover and strong northwesterly winds. The winds, unbeknown to the fliers, had set them some distance to the south of their course and considerably reduced their speed over the surface. As they passed through the front and emerged from the clouds, they saw land passing behind them and a great expanse of shallow water extending to the west as far as the eye could see. Assuming that they had just passed over the southern tip of the Florida mainland, their leader guided them in a big circle to the north, planning to approach Fort Lauderdale from the west. At this point they encountered seventy- to eighty-mile-an-hour head winds at eight thousand feet. On the northeast heading that they were bearing, they soon ran out of land and found that they were again over open ocean. They had confused Andros, the largest of the Bahama Islands, for south Florida.

It was at this point shortly before 4 P.M. that they radioed their base that they were lost. Attempting to retrace their flight pattern, they once again headed west. This would place them over the deep waters northeast of Andros. By now they were in contact with Radioman Baker. To the south they could see land, which they described to Baker. By the time the communications crew determined that the land was Andros, the flight was already half the distance back to Florida. The one plane whose pilot had cut out by himself had already departed from the group, leaving only four planes approaching the Florida coast. But for some strange reason the flight leader was still convinced that he was over the Gulf of Mexico and reversed direction. The flight was now continuing eastward and did so until all communications with the planes was lost. They flew on and on until one by one they ran out of fuel and crash-landed—some in Bahamian waters and others in the open Atlantic in an area sometimes referred to as the Sargasso Sea.

The facts that are known give proof to the fate that befell the aviators. But is the proof beyond all doubt? The two final links to the chain of events are still missing . . . the victims and the wreckage. One plane lost without a trace is completely possible. Two planes lost without a trace is still conceivable. Three planes . . . feasible, but not probable. But six aircraft and twenty-seven crewmen, and no two going down in the exact same location? This leaves the search and rescue teams six separate crash sites within or near a group of islands, and all the planes went down within a rel- atively short time span. Even if the huge Mariner had suffered a shattering explosion, it contained many bits and pieces that should have remained afloat. Had the Avengers been ripped apart in a violent squall—the "white water" theory—they too should have left some debris floating on the surface. And could the fifth Avenger that went off alone also have encoun- tered a squall? The five TBMs couldn't possibly ex- pend their fuel supplies at the same instant. Each one should have been able to "belly" in and stand a good chance of remaining afloat for at least several minutes. On numerous occasions during the war in the Pacific Avengers had force landed at sea and remained afloat long enough for their crews to inflate life rafts and "abandon ship" without getting their feet wet.

If it was the one in which Corporal Kosnar was to have flown, the fifth plane should have been able to remain aloft somewhat longer than the others as its load would have been lighter, and it could also have abandoned the formation before the head winds were encountered that caused the planes to expend more fuel than normal. This could well account for the mysterious "FT—FT" signal received by Opa Locka Tower several hours after all communication with the flight was lost. There were numerous islands between the closest area to Florida that the flight reached and the open sea to the east. It would seem probable that either the fifth plane or the formation would have passed at least one and made an attempted crash landing. Yet the possibility remains that the planes might have, by some twist of fate, flown eastward through the Bahamas over the one narrow corridor in the North West Providence Channel from which the fliers might not sight any islands. They would have had land about twelve miles away on either side. The land would have been the Berry Islands, the southern tip of Great Abaco, and the northern tip of Eleuthera Island . . . and after that the open sea.

In May, 1961, newspapers from New York to Florida headlined the speculation that "Fort Lauderdale's Great Sea Mystery Might At Last Be Solved." On May 19, a huge suction dredge was working in the Banana River on the western perimeter of Cape Canaveral. The purpose of the dredging was to obtain fill for the huge Saturn missile complex under construction at the cape. After days of working in the soft mud without any difficulty, the big suction pump suddenly growled and ground to a halt. Upon dismantling the machinery, the crew discovered that an aircraft engine cylinder had become lodged in the mechanism. At first, the men thought it might be from a junked plane. However, after removing the aluminum cylinder, they discovered human bones and a shoe later identified as being a typical navy or marine high-top flier's shoe. A team of divers was dispatched to the scene, but found the water so murky that they couldn't see their own bubbles. The bottom mud was so deep as to make their efforts completely useless.

It was determined that the cylinder was from a line type of aircraft such as an Avenger. Soon afterward the dredge brought up two identical radio panels of the type that might be found on an Avenger. The newspapers followed the story for almost a week, but the mystery was to remain unsolved. A navy team headed by Lieutenant Commander Richard Stack determined that the wreckage came from a navy SBD, an early World War II attack bomber. But now, a new mystery emerged. A search of records was unable to reveal any unaccounted for SBDs from World War II bases within that plane's flying range from the wreck site.

In the June, 1973, issue of *Naval Aviation News,* a government publication, there appeared an article by Michael McDonell called "Lost Patrol."

One of the questions that is answered is why Commander Cox, the senior flight instructor, didn't go back out again when he returned to the base after experiencing radio troubles. According to McDonell's article, Cox requested permission to take off in another plane in an attempt to assist the afflicted Avengers. However, the operations officer replied, "Very definitely, no." The operations officer stated at the Board of Inquiry that he felt that Flight 19 had finally reoriented itself and was returning to base. He also stated that there was a safety factor due to the bad weather that was moving in from the north. However, there is still no answer as to why the other eleven planes in Commander Cox's flight were unable to assist after he experienced communications trouble.

The communications with the planes and the messages passing between them and the ground station as told in the *Aviation Week* article tends to verify Radioman Melvin Baker's story. It also verifies Baker's feeling that the DF fix took unduly long to obtain. By the time the fix was obtained, the planes were far out to sea with only "about twenty minutes of fuel remaining." If a proper fix had been obtained in time, would the twenty-seven airmen have perished? The only ones who can answer this are dead. The article sheds new light on the missing PBM search plane. The aircraft carrier U.S.S. *Solomons,* which was operating off the Florida coast at the time the planes vanished, reported later, "Our air search radar showed a plane after takeoff from Banana River last night joining with another plane [the second search plane], then separating and proceeding on course 045 degrees at exact time S.S. *Gaines Mills* sighted flames and in exact spot the above plane disappeared from radar screen and never reappeared." This certainly lends credence to the theory that Lieutenant Cone's Mariner exploded in midair.

According to the article, another member of the flight besides Kosnar didn't feel that he should fly that day. He asked the duty officer to find another pilot, stating that he did not want to fly. However, he was told that no relief was available, and his request would have to be denied. Lieutenant Taylor's tardiness in reporting to the operations office delayed the flight's takeoff for twenty-five minutes. But fly he did —into oblivion.

2. In the Beginning

Shall I or shall I not warn him? After all, he did send me back home in chains and disgrace, did he not? Now, he is about to return to Spain, but as a hero. Is it fair? These may well have been the thoughts that passed through Christopher Columbus's mind as he stood in the stern sheets of the boat in which he was being rowed ashore at Santo Domingo on July 1, 1502. His thoughts were motivated by the sight of thirty-two caravels that had assembled and were being prepared for their voyage home to Spain. The wind was from out of the west. But it should have been from the east in the Caribbean during the summer months unless, as Columbus realized, it was before a storm of storms—a hurricane.

It was two years since Columbus had seen Bobadilla, the man who had sent him back to Spain in irons. But Columbus had been freed to return to the New World and continue his explorations in the western Caribbean. Now their paths would once again cross, because out of consideration for the more than eight hundred seamen who would be voyaging back to

Spain in that fleet, Columbus decided to warn
Bobadilla of the impending storm. He ordered the
oarsmen to head for the *El Dorado,* the flagship of
Admiral Antonio de Torres. Bobadilla was to sail on
that vessel. The wind was still blowing from the west.

As Columbus climbed aboard, he saw a group of
Indian slaves struggling with a table of solid gold—a
table that weighed over three thousand pounds. The
table was destined for the royal family of Spain as a
gift from Bobadilla. In addition to the priceless table,
the vessel was to carry two million dollars in gold and
silver. It would be the richest ship, yet, to return to
Spain.

Bobadilla, a passenger aboard the *El Dorado,* was
standing high up on the sterncastle. Unabashed, the
explorer approached the man who would have liked to
have seen him back in chains. He attempted to warn
Bobadilla of the looming tempest. But the retiring
governor of Hispaniola (the present-day Haiti and
the Dominican Republic) only scoffed at the warning
of his country's most experienced seaman. Although
Admiral de Torres considered Columbus's warning,
Bobadilla convinced him that the unusual west winds
would carry them far out into the Atlantic and save
them much of the time ordinarily lost encountering
the prevailing easterly head winds. That night, as the
great explorer stood on a hill watching, the fleet set
sail. By morning, the last of the ships had disappeared
over the horizon.

Three days later, as the armada entered the Mona
Passage, which separates Hispaniola from Puerto Rico,
the wrath of nature was loosed in all its fury. The seas
roared and the winds howled. Lightning flashed.
Thunder rumbled. Rain moved perpendicular to its
proper direction. Sails disintegrated. Masts snapped.
Men screamed. Others knelt down to pray. Tons of

gold and silver plummeted to the ocean floor through ruptured hulls. Then without warning the wind and rain were gone. All was still but the sea. The sun burst through wind-driven clouds. And half the fleet was no more.

The *El Dorado* was still afloat. Damaged, but God had spared her, so those on board thought. The air was hot, humid, and windless. The sea's surface was a mass distortion of liquid. Large swells rolled in from one direction. Larger ones came in from another quarter. And even greater seas moved in from a third point. Yet, the air was still windless. The sun was bright and hot. The caravels bobbed and tossed to such an extent that the movement continued the damage where the wind had left off. Repairs were impossible. Then as suddenly as the wind had stopped only minutes before, it returned from the opposite direction with a renewed fury. A fury that caught the surviving mariners completely unaware, for they had never before been through a West Indian hurricane.

Again lightning flashed, but there was no sound of thunder. The shrieking winds drowned it out. Paint was blasted from hulls and superstructures by the driving rain. Men were decapitated by torn rigging cracking about in winds the velocity of which defied measurement. More vessels succumbed to the fury, vessels that might have been saved had the crews kneeling in prayer put forth that effort to keep their ships afloat. Falling spars smashed men into the decks . . . men who would have died easier had they been washed overboard. Helmsmen who thought their ships were steering easier didn't know that the rudders were gone. Caravels smashed together and sank as one. Those who opened their eyes into the wind-driven rain had their eyeballs splattered out of the sockets. Clothes were ripped away, and bodies were masses of torn flesh as though they had been lashed and beaten by King Neptune's own master-at-arms. Mouths that opened to scream spewed forth blood instead of words. Cargoes shifted. Vessels capsized. Men were crushed. Others drowned. Those dying prayed to live. Those living prayed to die.

What could Bobadilla have been thinking? Could it have been of the solid gold table—the most esteemed piece of furniture the world had ever seen? Possibly he thought of his own safety or even the warning from Columbus that he had scorned. More than likely he was too busy struggling to survive to think of anything. But the world will never know. For the *El Dorado* and twenty-six other ships were no more when the winds began to abate at dusk that day. Ten wrecks were later found on reefs and along beaches on the shores of Puerto Rico and Hispaniola. Seventeen, with their crews, had completely vanished. Somewhere a thousand feet or more under the waters of the Mona Passage lies a thirty-one-hundred-pound solid gold table and what might be left of the caravel *El Dorado*. No trace of the seventeen little ships has ever been found. The crews of the five surviving vessels were too busy fighting for their lives to have taken notice.

The seventeen treasure-laden caravels that took their crews to oblivion on July 4, 1502, are the first known disappearances in the "Devil's Triangle." True, we know that there was a reason for their loss, but isn't there a reason for all of the hundreds of ships and planes and the thousands of people who disappeared down through the years since then in the "Devil's Triangle"?

3. To Beyond the
Wild Blue Yonder

Fly by the seat of their pants is what they did. Their airplanes were no more than fabric-covered crates. The fabric was stiffened with banana oil, which was referred to as "dope." In those days, only Buck Rogers covered his aircraft with metal. The smell of airplane dope was symbolic with the wings of man—skimming along over cornfields and treetops and flying off into the blue. Every schoolboy's ambition was to grow up and become a pilot. And those boys lucky enough to live near an airport or able to commute there on their bicycles would spend all day Saturday washing and wiping planes in exchange for a ten-minute ride in one on Sunday. The only event that topped going to the lake for a picnic was piling into the family jalopy after dinner on a summer evening or a Sunday afternoon and driving out to the country (all airports were located in the country in those days) to watch the planes taking off and landing. Every boy's hobby was building model airplanes whose rubber-band motors might carry them as far as a mile if wind and air conditions were just

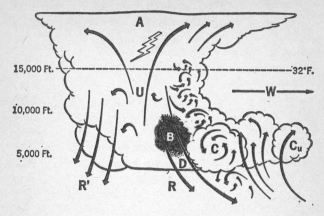

Key to Diagram of Cumulonimbus Cloud

A —Anvil Top   U —Up Drafts
B —Dark Area   R —Primary Rain Area
C —Roll Cloud   R'—Secondary Area
Cᵤ—Advance Cumulus Cloud   W—Wind Direction
D —Down Drafts

It is very easy to understand from this diagram what
havoc can be encountered by an aircraft flying
through a thunder cloud.
(*Courtesy of Aviation Training Division, U.S. Navy*)

right. The biggest event of the year was not the circus
or the fair. It was the air show. Every boy wanted to
change places with those daredevil barnstorming
pilots who lived such fast and exciting lives. They
flew upside down just a few feet above the ground,
crashed through burning buildings, pulled out of tail-
spins at the last second, and roared past the grand-
stands with pretty girls dressed like cowboys standing
on the wings.

But there was also another, though less well-known,
breed of aviators leading daredevil lives. These pilots
were the jaunty flying rumrunners. No less than forty-
five of them operated between West End in the

Bahamas and Palm Beach in the late twenties and early thirties. When the government agencies enforcing the National Prohibition Act finally obtained vessels as fast as those used by the "rummies," as the rumrunners were called, the latter took to the air.

Grand Bahama is the second largest of the Bahama Islands. At its western tip is West End, which is fifty miles east of Palm Beach. And at West End is where John Smith, a native Bahamian, maintained his business concern. The establishment was called the First and Last Bar. And it was from John Smith's firm that most of the illicit air cargo was acquired. The liquor was packed six bottles to a burlap sack, and two sacks made a case. Smith's enterprise provided a livelihood for twenty-two Bahamian girls, who did nothing but sew bottles of whiskey into sacks for shipment. A Model-T Ford truck would then carry the contraband to one of several landing strips hacked out of the pine forests southeast of the town. The pilots received ten dollars per case for flying the liquor to one of a number of isolated landing fields in western Palm Beach County. They would pack so many bags of whiskey in their planes that they could only see straight ahead.

One of these flying rumrunners, Al Page (his name has been changed as he is still alive), recalled the time he was cruising along in a float-equipped seaplane about fifty feet above the water during rough weather. A gasoline line broke, and he was forced to land in the choppy seas. Upon impact, the pontoons broke off, and the plane nosed over sinking almost immediately due to the weight of its cargo. Al barely had time to climb out.

A rum-running boat en route to Palm Beach saw the crash landing and pulled up alongside the swimming pilot who asked for a lift to Florida. The boat's captain, who knew Al, climbed over the many cases of whiskey that had lowered the boat far down below its waterline. He called out, "Al, before we can take you aboard, we'll have to ditch six cases of champagne. Will you pay for the champagne? Otherwise, you've got yourself a long swim!" Needless to say, Al paid for those six cases of champagne. If the rum-running boat had not seen Al, the evening's headlines would have read something like "Pilot and Seaplane Disappear at Sea."

Herbie Pond was another flying rumrunner. Herbie wasn't as lucky as Al Page. In June, 1931, Herbie came flying in from West End with a full load of whiskey and just clearing the palm trees and Australian pines lining the Palm Beach oceanfront. Crossing Lake Worth, he continued on past West Palm Beach and out into the boondocks to an area now occupied by the West Palm Beach exit of the Sunshine State Parkway. In 1931, it was a cow pasture and rendezvous point for bootleggers and planes smuggling liquor in from West End. It was a bright sunny afternoon with a light prevailing southeasterly breeze blowing. Herbie circled the pasture several times to be sure that no revenuers were waiting for him to land. As he circled, two Hudson Super Six touring cars (the bootleggers' favorite) and a big seven-passenger Packard Super Eight sedan pulled out onto the field. They were Herbie's clients. The Curtiss Robin high-winged monoplane made a perfect three-point landing. Herbie was a most skilled pilot, and the Curtiss Robin was one of the most dependable airplanes.

Before the seven-cylinder radial engine stopped turning, the men from the cars had started unloading the plane. Hand to hand they passed the bags into the first car. When it was loaded, the second Hudson took its place as the unloading continued uninterrupted. The men in the Packard would guard the other two cars. As soon as the plane was emptied of its forty-four sacks of whiskey (twenty-two cases), Herbie checked the oil and fuel levels, inspected the plane's mechanisms, climbed aboard, and yelled, "Switch off." One of the men cranked the propeller over slowly. On the second turn of the prop, the engine fired up. Herbie waved to the men who were putting the tops up on the Hudsons and taxied to the northwest corner of the field. As the three cars started to move off, Herbie revved the engine, and the plane roared across the pasture and rose smoothly into the air and over the treetops toward the ocean, West End, another cargo of whiskey, and the "Devil's Triangle." That was the last that was ever seen of the Curtiss Robin and Herbie Pond, the man who has the distinction of being the first known aviator to have vanished in the "Devil's Triangle."

In December, 1935, three Cubans, Jose Perez, Juan Hernandez, and Jose Delgado, took off from Havana in their newly acquired plane. They were flying to the Isle of Pine one hundred miles to the south to look at some real estate holdings. The four-passenger closed Waco biplane was one of the most reliable airplanes of its day. With its big 250 horsepower Wright Whirlwind engine, the plane should have taken no more than one hour to reach its destination. The first forty miles would be over land, and the rest of the flight would be over crystal-clear water no more than twenty-five feet deep. Even the poorest of navigators could reach the thirty-five-mile-wide island without deviating from the shallow waters that separated it from Cuba. Perez was an experienced aviator. Yet, they never reached their destination.

The next day a search was commenced that took in all of the land area south of Havana. Searchers on foot explored every mountainside and peak. Planes and boats scoured the glass-smooth waters that the missing plane would have flown over. No trace of the Waco biplane or the three men was ever found. They had flown into "El Triangle del Diablo."

During World War II a number of military planes disappeared in the "triangle." Most of the losses were not made public. Many of the planes were flown by student pilots, which might account for some of the casualties. In fact, even in recent years hunters and construction workers have found the remains of unidentifiable planes, both military and civilian, far back in the Florida Everglades. Some of the planes had never been listed as missing. For every plane reported as having been lost in the area of the "Devil's Triangle," there are at least two that have gone unreported—at least as far as the public is concerned. But those with a significant loss of life usually do make the headlines.

In December, 1944, a group of seven United States bombers en route to Italy as replacements for battered groups of the Fifteenth Air Force stopped over in Bermuda.

After fueling and a rest for the crews, the planes took off. Within two hours, some three hundred miles out of Kindley Field, the flight encountered a series of freak weather phenomena. The planes bounced around for less than a minute, but some of them were swept upward and dropped down for hundreds of feet. So bad was the turbulence that two of the planes were forced to return to Bermuda. The other five were never seen again. This was almost one year to the day before the five Navy planes flew off into oblivion from Fort Lauderdale Naval Air Station.

Little has been released on the disappearance of the

five Air Force bombers, nor has much been written about it. In his book *Invisible Horizons,* Vincent Gaddis does give an eyewitness account from a survivor of one of the two planes that made it back to Kindley Field.

However, two incidents that have received a considerable amount of play in both newspaper and magazine articles also took place near Bermuda. At 10:30 P.M. on January 30, 1948, a message was radioed to Kindley Field. It was from Captain D. Colby, pilot of the British South American Airlines (since absorbed by BOAC) airliner *Star Tiger.* "Position approximately four hundred miles northeast of you. Expect to arrive on schedule. Weather and performance excellent."

The airliner had departed London on Tuesday, January 27, and stopped at both Lisbon, Portugal, and Santa Maria in the Azore Islands. The *Star Tiger* was to stop at Bermuda and Nassau on its flight to Kingston, Jamaica. At the time of Captain Colby's message, the plane was carrying twenty-five passengers and a crew of six. Among the passengers was the fifty-three-year-old British air marshal, Sir Arthur Coningham. The *Star Tiger* was due to land in Bermuda shortly before midnight. But after Captain Colby's 10:30 message, the plane was never heard from again.

By dawn the following morning, Colonel Tom Ferguson, commander of the United States Air Force Base at Kindley Field had thirty planes and ten ships searching for the *Star Tiger* or survivors from the plane. On January 31, bad weather imperiled all hope for the missing airliner. Severe storms and high seas were prevalent throughout the search area. After the weather moved off, eleven hundred men participated in the renewed search. But on Tuesday, February 4, the search was over. No survivors, wreckage, or victims were found. That same day amateur radio operators along the east coast of the United States picked up the message "Tiger." A short while later a voice spelled out the letters "G-A-H-N-P." This was strange, for the *Star Tiger's* call letters were G-A-H-N-P. Immediately, the search was resumed. But no one was able to get a position fix on the source of the signals; thus, officials decided that the mysterious messages were a hoax.

The *Star Tiger* was a Tudor IV, an airliner ahead of its time. A modification of the British Lancaster of World War II fame, the Tudor IV was powered by four 1,760 horsepower Rolls-Royce Merlin 623 engines. Its speed was 235 miles per hour at sea level and 305 at twenty-five thousand feet. The Tudor's main cabin was pressurized and had six emergency exits in addition to the main doors. There were accommodations for thirty-two passengers plus the crew. A number of airlines, including BOAC, ordered Tudor IVs for passenger service and modified versions for air cargo transports. Assembly lines at Avro, the plane's builder, worked around the clock. But as the bells of the New Year rang in 1949, they tolled the death knell for the Tudor as a passenger plane.

The morning of January 19, 1949, was a beautiful morning in Bermuda, one of those mornings that make one want to stay outdoors rather than go to work. And that is how air controller Henry White felt as he drove up to the tower at Kindley Field on his motor scooter. It was 7:45 A.M. He had a few minutes before his eight o'clock report time. He walked over to the fence and watched a British South American Airlines Tudor IV airliner, the *Star Ariel*, revving her engines at the far end of the field. The pilot gunned the powerful engines, the plane roared down the run-

way and lifted into the air. The surrounding hills and
buildings reverberated to the pulsation of the four engines.

At 8:25 A.M., the *Star Ariel's* pilot, Captain J. C.
McPhee, radioed Bermuda tower, "We're approximately 180 miles south of Bermuda now. Flying
weather is fair. Everything is fine. I am changing
radio frequency to Nassau." That is the last that anyone ever heard of the *Star Ariel*, its seven crew members, and thirteen passengers. Once again, as ideal
flying weather prevailed in the "Devil's Triangle," another airplane without any indication of distress flew
off into the unknown.

When the Tudor IV failed to arrive in Nassau, a
massive search was initiated. At the time the U.S.Navy
was conducting manuevers in an area several hundred
miles south of Bermuda. The ships and planes were
diverted from the training exercise to the search.
Among the vessels participating were the battleship
Missouri, the aircraft carriers *Leyte* and *Kearsage*, a
number of cruisers and destroyers, and several auxiliary ships. They searched from Bermuda to Jamaica.
Two destroyers rushed to a point three hundred miles
south of Bermuda where both a commercial airliner
and a United States Air Force bomber reported seeing a strange green light on the water. The destroyers
found nothing. Soon the search pattern overlapped
that of a coast guard search for a fishing boat, the
Driftwood, that had vanished on a trip from Fort
Lauderdale to Bimini with five men aboard. No trace
of the *Driftwood* or *Star Ariel* was ever found.

As a result of the unexplained disappearances of the
two Tudor IVs, plus the loss of a third one off the
coast of South America, the minister of civil aviation
in England decreed that the Tudor IV should no longer be used on passenger routes. Those remaining were

converted to cargo carriers and performed valuable service on the Berlin Airlift. Production on new Tudor IVs ceased. The only information released concerning the *Star Tiger* and the *Star Ariel* was that they each apparently crashed into the ocean without shattering and sank to the bottom of the sea in one piece.

Chico, California, is a long way from the "Devil's Triangle." There the New Tribes Mission, an inter-denominational organization that trained missionaries for out-of-the-way posts, had its headquarters and training facilities. The mission even owned a DC-3 airliner, used to convey the missionaries to their stations.

On June 9, 1950, after a twenty-four-hour layover following a flight from northern California, the mission's plane took off from Miami, Florida. Her destination was Venezuela with a fuel stop at Jamaica. David Kimball of Chicago was the mission's staff copilot, and his wife Hazel was the stewardess. Piloting the DC-3 was Captain Ben Wetherald, who was also a missionary. Mildred Garber, Clyde Snow, and John Greiner, members of the mission's staff at Chico, were among the passengers. The other passengers were missionaries and their children including Harold Mills; William Hoffman and his wife Peggy, plus their two children Lorel and Billy; and Mrs. Betty Hilker with her three children Nelda, Danny, and David.

The missionary plane made a fuel stop at Kingston and took off for Maracaibo, a destination that it never reached. A week transpired before the plane was reported overdue. By then the plane had flown into the unknown taking fifteen people to meet the God whose word they planned to spread among the tribesmen in the jungles of South America.

On February 2, 1953, an SOS was received from a British York transport plane carrying thirty-three passengers and a crew of six en route to Jamaica. The troop carrier's signal gave no position or reason for the distress call. Two weeks of intensive searching revealed no clue as to the fate of the plane or victims. A Royal Air Force Court of Inquiry stated that the cause was "unascertainable."

A navy Constellation carrying forty-two persons including wives and children of service personnel vanished northwest of Bermuda on October 30, 1954. More than a hundred planes and ships searched for days, but no trace of the big four-engined Connie or those who had been aboard it was found. The navy could offer no explanation as to the disappearance.

On the night of Friday, November 9, 1956, a twin-engine navy P5M patrol bomber roared skyward from Hamilton, Bermuda. The plane was a modification of the Martin Mariner retaining an identical wing and upper hull and was equipped with a special magnetic anomaly detector. A radio message was transmitted from the plane shortly after it was airborne. Nothing else was ever heard from the Martin P5M or the ten men aboard her. A Liberian cargo ship in the area reported seeing a burning aircraft about 9 P.M. A search of the area was made, but again, the same story—no survivors, no bodies, no wreckage.

Although the following incident didn't occur in the area referred to as the "Devil's Triangle," it did happen close enough to merit mention. It was a raw cold winter morning on January 8, 1962, when the ground crew pulled the chocks out from the wheels of the huge air force KB-50 tanker at Langley Air Force Base, Virginia, as the plane was prepared to take off on a fueling operation. The KB-50 was a modification of the last Super Fortresses built. Although they were classed as jet-boosted flight-refueling tankers, they were actually propeller-driven planes. As the flying tanker reached the runway, the tower controller gave the pilot, Major Robert Tawney, the OK to take off. A short time later, the tower picked up a distorted distress signal from the plane. A search was under way within minutes, but no trace of the KB-50 or the eight airmen aboard was ever found.

Now that you've read of propeller-driven aircraft vanishing in this mysterious sector of the Atlantic Ocean, you are probably thinking of the possible mishaps that the planes might have encountered—freak weather, human error, oceanic aberration, magnetic anomaly, structural or mechanical malfunction. It could have been any or all of these—or something else. But what about jet aircraft capable of flying above any interference created by an oceanic phenomenon? On August 28, 1963, the "Devil's Triangle" entered the jet age.

Two KC-135 strato-tankers stationed with the Nineteenth Bomber Wing of the Strategic Air Command at Homestead Air Force Base, Florida, taxied to take off. Basically a military version of the 707 jetliner, the strato-tankers were to be the first two jet aircraft to add their names to the ambiguous chronicle of the "Devil's Triangle." Eleven crewmen were aboard the two planes. Their destination, when they lifted skyward, was secret.

At noon the planes radioed their position as 335 miles southwest of Bermuda—then silence. All attempts to contact the planes failed. And once again a massive air-sea search was under way. But this time evidence was found. A substantial amount of KC-135 wreckage was located not far from the planes' last reported position. One search pilot described the area as "a floating junkyard." The coast guard cutter *Owasco* arrived at the scene to collect the debris. On August 29, the Associated Press reported that three life rafts—each plane would have carried two of this type —had been found. Continued searching revealed no survivors or bodies. It was assumed that the planes, flying in formation as ordered, were the victims of a midair collision, and the search was called off.

However, less than forty-eight hours later on August 31, a second concentration of KC-135 wreckage was found—but 160 miles away from the first crash site in an area approximately 400 miles east of Fort Pierce. The coast guard cutter *Chiola* was at the location, but was having communication difficulties, which presented a mystery in itself, for the cutter had the most modern equipment. Could whatever was affecting the *Chiola*'s radios have had something to do with the loss of the two planes?

The two KC-135s had been flying in formation and were in constant sight of each other both visually and with radar. They were communicating with each other periodically by radio until they went off the air right after their last position report. Why didn't the remaining plane radio a distress message when the first plane went down? Why were three life rafts found at one of the crash sites when there should have been but two?

Although the wreckage from both locations was definitely ascertained as being from the two missing planes through the identification of certain wreckage including one of the flier's stenciled helmets, there was still no explanation for the distance between the two crash areas. Could they have been in one of the "triangle's" radio "skip zones" or "dead zones" where atmospheric conditions render communication sets inoperable? Was the radio phenomena still occurring when the *Chiola* reached the second crash site? These "zones" are known to exist. But their effects are limited to areas of a few miles and not the distance that separated the two clusters of KC-135 debris. The second plane should have been in a clear zone in a matter of minutes after the first one went down. Also the radio frequencies could have been switched to other channels, for the "dead zones" affect only certain wavelengths, and a channel affected one day could be unaffected the following day. Military surface vessels and aircraft can switch both frequencies and antennae to cope with the "dead zones."

Some UFO buffs theorized that a third aircraft of unknown origin jammed both planes' radios and destroyed the first plane. The second one managed to fly over 150 miles before it too was caught and destroyed.

Probably the most plausible explanation is that the two aircraft had malfunctions of their oxygen or pressurization systems within minutes of each other as a result of attaining too great an altitude or from mechanical failure. There are documented cases of this having happened to military jets in which the crews had succumbed, and the planes flew on for several hours on their automatic pilots before crashing. Even though only a conjecture, this seems to be the only reasonable explanation of why one of the aircraft couldn't transmit some sort of signal during its last 160 miles.

It seems apparent that something happened to the crews of the two KC-135s before the planes went down. But the question remains, Where did the third life raft come from at the first crash scene?

Forty-one-year-old Louis Giuntoli was an air force veteran of both World War II and Korea. After his release from active duty, he returned to Milwaukee where he made his living as a self-employed salesman. He lived with his wife and son in the suburb of Brookfield. Twenty-nine-year-old Larry Gares was a graduate student at the University of Wisconsin's Milwaukee Branch as was thirty-two-year-old Dick Bassett. Milton Adams, thirty-six; Tom Nugent, thirty; Frank Ellison, forty-one; Raoul Benedict, thirty-five; Duane Brooks, thirty-two; and Norman Mimier, thirty-four, all lived in or around Milwaukee. John Lazenby was visiting his mother at the Isla Gold Trailer Park in Miami. He was an airman first class home on leave from Ramey Air Force Base, Puerto Rico. These ten men had one thing in common—the headlines of the June 7, 1965, *Miami Herald,* which read: "Plane from Homestead Missing off Bahamas."

The events that led to these headlines began as Major Louis Giontoli winged his C-119 air force reserve cargo plane skyward from Milwaukee's General Mitchell Field at 10 A.M. on Saturday, June 5, 1965. His copilot was Lieutenant Lawrence Gares. Both were air force reservists as were the other seven men aboard the flying boxcar. Their mission was to deliver and install a replacement engine for another C-119 from their squadron (the 440th Troop Carrier Wing) that was grounded at the air force installation on Grand Turk Island with an inoperative engine. Four of the nine men were technicians who were to change the engines. There was to be one stop en route. That was for fuel at Homestead Air Force Base, Florida.

At 7:47 that evening the twin-engine plane left Homestead for Grand Turk. Ten men were aboard, as Airman Lazenby had hitched a ride for the first leg of the journey back to his base in Puerto Rico. Ideal flying conditions prevailed at the time of take-off. But as the flying boxcar penetrated farther into the "twilight zone" of the Atlantic, thundershower activity increased. The storms were scattered enough for the plane to fly around them. The route being flown was designated as "Yankee" by the air force. It was the assigned air corridor for military aircraft flying between Homestead and Puerto Rico and island bases in between. The C-119 was due to land at Grand Turk at 11 P.M.

At 10:04 the plane radioed its position as being near Crooked Island. At about the same time, another C-119, flying northwest bound for Florida, flew through the same area. Its crew later reported thundershowers "with a lot of lightning."

Shortly after 10:30, the tower operator at Grand Turk picked up a garbled radio transmission originating from somewhere northeast of the island. Whether the transmission came from Major Giontoli's plane will never be known. At 11:45 P.M. the Miami coast guard was notified that the C-119 was overdue at Grand Turk.

By first light Sunday, the coast guard, air force, and navy had thirteen planes searching a two-thousand-square-mile area north of Grand Turk. Nothing was sighted. Seven planes continued to search through the night. On Monday, thirty-three planes and seven surface ships extended the search area beyond San Salvador Island to the north and the Dominican Republic to the south. The search covered seventy-seven thousand square miles.

The missing plane would have exhausted its fuel

supply by 4:30 Sunday morning. But it is highly unlikely that it was aloft that long, for it could have
radioed during that time, or even flown back to Homestead with the fuel remaining at the time it was reported overdue. The C-119 carried a twenty-man life
raft that could have been spotted easily from the air.
At the time it was presumed lost, sea conditions were
ideal for ditching an aircraft. However, Colonel Leon-
ard Dereszynski, vice-commander of the 440th
stated, "No one has ever ditched a C-119 at sea. In
fact, it isn't even recommended in the book."

"If the plane had exploded in the air, there would
have been something of it floating somewhere," said
Captain Hardy F. Lebel, one of the search pilots.
"And if it was in one piece until it crashed, it would
break up on impact with the water, and debris, again,
would be seen. If the plane did not explode in the
water, somebody would have gotten out."

Lebel and his crew sighted a flashing light Monday
night. It turned out to be an off-course fishing boat.
Later they saw a flare, but it turned out to be an
illusion. Tuesday night the search was greatly hampered by bad weather passing through the area.

One pilot stated that Giontoli might have been put
off course by radio jammings from Cuba that cause
radio navigation instruments to malfunction. Other pilots had experienced this.

Meanwhile, back in Milwaukee, Mrs. Dorothy Giontoli, the major's wife, described the waiting as terrible.
But she said, "All you can do is hope and be optimistic
about it."

Technical Sergeant Norman Mimier's wife said,
"He's got to come back."

Mrs. Frank Ellison, the master sergeant's wife,
stated, "We're sure God will take care of him."

The wife of Master Sergeant Milton Adams thought

tearfully out loud, "It doesn't seem like it's true. It seems like it can't happen. It just can't happen."

Navigator Captain Richard Bassett's wife said that the uncertainty about her husband's fate was difficult to endure. "I am completely numb," she said. "I can't think. I know they're doing everything they can."

Another wife said, "There isn't anything anyone can do. It's just a matter of waiting."

At 8 P.M. on Thursday, June 10, when flying box-car number 25889 touched down at Ramey Air Force Base after hours of searching for its missing sister plane from the 440th, the search was called off. Major Harry Anderson, of Minneapolis, and his crew had searched thousands of square miles of ocean along with the other planes. All of the planes reported finding nothing of significance. The coast guard in Miami called off the search with a statement that was right to the point: "Five days and nights of searching. Results negative. There are no conjectures." Chief George Schiffer from the Public Information Office of the Seventh Coast Guard District said that the case would not be closed until some indication of the fate of the missing plane was found.

"Death Plane Clue Found At Sea" was the Miami *News*'s headline two months later on August 17. The coast guard cutter *Diligence* reported that a wheel and other items stenciled with the lost C-119's number, 2860, were found. Further investigation revealed that the parts were definitely from a C-119 and not a hoax. Plane number 2860 was the only C-119 missing at the time. Deterioration and marine growth indicated that the items were immersed in the sea no more than two months. There was no indication as to what happened to the plane. The ten men were presumed to be dead. Many opinions and theories have been expressed concerning the missing C-119. Down through the years, a number of writers of stories about the "triangle" have merely listed the loss as another strange incident. However, until the day when the sea gives up its secret of the C-119's fate, one can only go by what the coast guard release said on the last day of the search: "Results negative. There are no conjectures."

On January 11, 1967, photographer Oscar Barber assisted in the loading of motion picture equipment and other related supplies aboard a converted Chase YC-122 cargo plane. The plane was basically a large glider with a pair of engines added to make it a theoretically safe and stable aircraft. The plane was loaded at Fort Lauderdale International Airport, where the five planes of the ill-fated Flight 19 took off twenty-two years earlier. The cargo was destined for an Ivan Tors movie studio film unit on location at Bimini sixty miles across the Gulf Stream.

Charles Lundgren was the pilot and William Suiter his copilot. Both were from Fort Lauderdale. Two passengers going along "just for the ride" were Larry Waplehorst, a motel owner, and Eugene Lemire, an off-duty airline pilot. Barber was to be the third passenger. However, at the last minute, he decided not to fly on that plane. He watched the plane climb high up over the Atlantic and then went home.

The perfectly sound aircraft with experienced pilots aboard sent one routine radio message back to Fort Lauderdale tower—then vanished somewhere along that sixty-mile stretch of open water. Debris was found thirty miles northwest of Bimini but was never substantiated as being from the missing cargo plane.

Asked later why he didn't go on the flight, Barber said, "I just had a feeling that I should go by commercial airliner." Could Oscar Barber have had the same feeling that Allen Kosnar had at that same air field back in December, 1945, when Flight 19 was preparing to take off?

The disappearance of the four men and their plane-load of motion picture equipment was only the beginning of a chain of tragic events that labeled the week of January 11 through January 18, 1967, as a black week for Caribbean and Florida aviation. On the same day that the Chase Y-122 vanished, fifty-five-year-old Phillip Quigley disappeared in his light plane on a flight from Cozumel to Honduras. He had filed a flight plan, but because of international clearance delays, his disappearance was not noted for four days.

Three days later on the morning of Saturday, January 14, Robert Van Westerborg, a thirty-five-year-old Miami business consultant, was busily checking over his single-engine Beechcraft Bonanza at Miami International Airport. Van Westerborg was known to local Federal Aviation Agency officials as one of the staunchest advocates of flight safety. He attended aviation safety meetings regularly and lectured to fellow pilots on the importance of filing a flight plan. He said, "Flight plans have saved more pilots than can be counted. If a plane is more than fifteen minutes late, the FAA at once begins tracking it down."

At 12:22 P.M. Van Westerborg took off. Accompanying him were his wife Adelaide and two friends, Phillip de Berard, Jr., a public relations man for Southern Bell Telephone Company, and his wife.

One-half hour later the blue-and-white plane set down at the Ocean Reef Yacht Club's private three-thousand-foot landing strip on Key Largo. The group had lunch at the club's dining room and went back to the plane. They were planning to fly down along the Florida Keys to photograph the site of the telephone company's new microwave relay station. They were to return to Miami later that afternoon. A waitress found a camera on the table where the four had dined and a bellhop ran with it out to the plane. He handed it to a "tall man with glasses" just as the engine was being started. The plane took off.

A man and his wife who were out fishing later reported seeing a small blue-and-white plane taking off at Key Largo. It nosed out to sea. The aircraft and all four aboard were never seen again.

After seven days, the search was called off. Robert Van Westerborg, the man who said, "Flight plans have saved more pilots than can be counted," took off that day without filing a flight plan.

While the search for the missing Miami and Fort Lauderdale planes was going on far to the northwest and Quigley's plane was being hunted in the western Caribbean, fifty-two-year-old John D. Walston barreled his twin-engine Piper Apache down the runway at San Juan's international airport. As the ground gave way beneath him, he climbed and pointed the plane toward Saint Thomas in the Virgin Islands less than one hour's flying time away. His two passengers, who chartered the plane, were Mr. and Mrs. Stephan R. Currier. Thirty-three-year-old Mrs. Currier, the daughter of David Bruce, the United States ambassador to Great Britain, was heir to seven hundred million dollars. Her thirty-six-year-old husband was a philanthropist and champion of the Civil Rights movement. Their three children had been left at home while they took a ten-day West Indian vacation. They were flying to Saint Thomas to charter a yacht for a Caribbean cruise—a flight that would always be over or in sight of land as they would be able to see Puerto Rico until just before they reached Saint Thomas. But somewhere along that forty-mile stretch of open water something happened. The plane never reached Saint Thomas.

No trace of the missing two-engine plane or its three occupants was found during the seven-day search by forty military and civilian planes and a number of surface craft, a search that didn't get under way until nine hours after the missing plane should have landed. John Walston, who had been flying since before World War II and flew the route between San Juan and Saint Thomas many times, had for the first (and last) time not filed a flight plan.

There are numerous incidents of planes that didn't file a flight plan vanishing in the "triangle." But how many aircraft have there been that disappeared and have never been missed at all—planes that to this day are not listed as missing?

For example, take an eerie incident that occurred on March 23, 1969, involving a twin-engine Beechcraft being flown from Kingston, Jamaica, to Nassau by two Florida doctors. On that Saturday night, a Canadian military plane flying through the Bahamas picked up an urgent distress message from the doctors' plane. The doctors, James Horton and Charles Griggs, were from Okeechobee, Florida. They were returning to Palm Beach airport and were scheduled to refuel in Nassau. But something occurred before they landed at Nassau. In a search centered sixty miles northeast of Nassau, five coast guard planes covered thirteen thousand square miles on the first day. After five days, fifty thousand square miles had been searched. On the third day a fisherman reported seeing wreckage of an airplane on an island thirty miles northeast of Cuba.

Investigators went to the island and found an eight-foot-long section of an aircraft fuselage. The island was along the doctors' intended route. But two things didn't jive. The twin Beechcraft was already 120 miles past the island when the distress call was transmitted, and the wreckage was from a plane of a different color and type.

On March 27, the search was called off, and all hope was given up for the missing doctors whose mysterious disappearance evolved into a second mystery. Where did the wreckage that washed ashore on the island come from? There was no other known plane missing at that time, nor had any been lost during the previous months that would have matched the wreckage. Could it have been the wreckage of a phantom plane?

Less than three months later, a twenty-four-year-old Miami Beach nurse, Caroline Coscio, took off in her Cessna 172 from the air park at Pompano Beach, Florida. She and her passenger, Richard Rosen of North Miami Beach, were flying to Jamaica. After an uneventful flight to Nassau, they put down for fuel. They took off and proceeded to Georgetown in the Exumas for their second fuel stop. At 4:40 P.M., the Cessna was again airborne and heading for Grand Turk, its next gas stop.

At 7:35 P.M., the tower operator on Grand Turk received a message from the woman pilot that she was lost and her radio direction finder was on the blink. Guests staying at a hotel on a nearby island saw lights of a plane circling a short distance offshore at the time the tower was in contact with Miss Coscio. They had no idea that the plane was in trouble. At 8:22 P.M., the tower operator heard a panic message from the Cessna. "I'm out of fuel! I'm going down!" Then silence. Although this incident seems like another situation of a plane going down at sea after exhausting its fuel supply, it still is surrounded by an air of mystery. The hotel guests could see the Cessna's lights, but why couldn't Miss Coscio see the lights on the island, which were much brighter than those on her plane? The natural thing for her to do if she were lost and low on fuel would be to stay near the lights. But for some strange reason, she flew off into the darkness never to be seen again.

Four months later, Mr. and Mrs. Hector Guzman of Summit Hills, Puerto Rico, were returning home from Fort Lauderdale in their twin-engine light plane. After refueling at Great Inagua Island, they took off and headed east toward San Juan. The plane, equipped with both life jackets and rafts, was never seen again. Two more people had become victims of some unknown direful circumstance.

On July 26, 1971, six aircraft had terminated their search of eighty-two-thousand square miles of West Indian waters for a missing plane owned by Horizon Hunters Flying Club of Miami. The search was centered in an area forty miles west of Barbados. Aboard the missing plane were Paul and Dolores Warren of North Miami and Jerome and Leatrice Levin of North Miami Beach. They had been on a pleasure flight from Curaçao to Barbados. They radioed that they were ditching at sea, and the plane was never heard from again.

It is difficult to contemplate these incidents involving lost aircraft without *some* thought leaning toward the supernatural. Is there something strange and occult happening to the aircraft that are disappearing in the "triangle"? Strange—yes. But occult—no, or so says Ted Jones, a block layer in Miami. When Jones isn't building houses, he works at his hobby—classic airplanes. Ted owns and has restored a World War II T-6 trainer. It is a powerful low-wing, two-passenger single-engine plane. During the fall of 1969, Ted took off from Bimini in the Bahamas for Miami—forty-five miles across the Gulf Stream. The yellow plane roared into the air and headed due west.

As Jones approached the Florida coast, he ran into an extensive cloud cover. When the plane emerged from the clouds thirty minutes later, Jones found that he was not over Florida as he should have been. *He was back over Bimini.* His plane was still heading west. Were Jones and his T-6 airplane suspended in a time warp or another dimension for half an hour? "Not hardly," said Ted. "I had run into 175-mile-per-hour head winds and for thirty minutes I was blown backwards at fifty miles per hour."

There are probably a great variety of reasons for the loss of the dozens and dozens of aircraft that have flown into the "triangle" never to return. But, without doubt, the greatest single cause is running out of fuel after becoming lost or disoriented. Unless one has actually been out in those waters, it is difficult to realize what a vast empty expanse they are. And if a pilot is lost, how does he radio the position where he is ditching? And, too, how can one delve deeply into this subject on a rational basis if there were no witnesses?

But what if there were witnesses? Back in 1935 at Daytona Beach, Florida, hundreds of people saw a plane plunge into the surf just off shore—a plane that the authorities denied ever existed. (Detailed elsewhere in this book.) There have been other happenings too.

On Friday, September 10, 1971, an air force F-4 Phantom II jet fighter carrying Captain John Romero of Lafayette, Louisiana, and Lieutenant Norman Nor-

thrup of Portland, Oregon, took off from Homestead
Air Force Base at 8:05 A.M. The plane carried seventy
minutes of fuel. Four technicians watched the jet
fighter on the scope in their radar shack. Their bear-
ings fixed the jet's position as eighty-five miles southeast of Miami, which would place it over the western
edge of the Great Bahama Bank in the vicinity of
Orange Cay where the water is no more than thirty
feet deep. Then, suddenly, the "blip" representing
the plane on the radar screen disappeared. Within
minutes other jets were screaming down toward the
last known coordinates of the missing plane. The
coast guard cutter *Steadfast*, four coast guard planes,
and three from the air force searched a 22,600
mile area. But there was no sighting of the aircraft
or the two men aboard. An airborne magnetometer
was flown over the last location known. Readings
were picked up. Divers went down. But no trace of
the missing F-4 was found. The magnetometer had
revealed other wrecks (of boats) hitherto unknown.

But what about actual eyewitnesses. Witnesses who
were there and were able to give a firsthand report?
On October 20, 1971, the oceanographic research vessel
R/V Discoverer was taking bottom soundings thirteen miles south of Great Inagua Island.

Frank Bacahanov, Mario Alvarez, Rene Travieso, all
of Miami, and Hector Reales of Columbia were flying
overhead in a four-engine Super Constellation cargo
plane loaded with frozen sides of beef. Only a minute
or two after the plane passed over the *Discoverer*,
the research ship's crew saw it suddenly plummet
down in a horizontal spin and smash into the sea.
Within fifteen minutes, the vessel was at the site of
the crash. Yet, with all its sophisticated electronic
detecting gear it was unable to locate one piece of

wreckage from the big cargo plane. There were no bodies or even an oil slick. Just a side of beef floating on the surface. Had the *Discoverer* not been present when the Connie went down, there again would have been another chapter added to the legend of the "Triangle of Death."

It was a typical bright sunny morning along south Florida's west coast on Friday, May 25, 1973. The sky was cloudless, and the winds were light and south-easterly. As a rule, rains and thundershowers originate over the hot and humid interior, and don't reach the coastal areas until midafternoon. Thus, mornings are the ideal time to fly over the Florida peninsula in a light plane.

Forty-six-year-old Robert Corner waved good-bye to his wife. Reno Rigon smiled at his waving girl friend, Jean Gimble. Corner taxied the black-and-white Navion 16 away from the hangar area and out to the runway. The Fort Myers tower operator gave the OK to take off. The low-wing single-engine plane roared down the field and climbed skyward carrying the two men across the state to West Palm Beach.

After an uneventful flight, the Navion set down at West Palm Beach where Corner topped off the fuel tanks. He gave the plane a final check-over. The next leg of their flight to the Bahama Islands was over open water—more than fifty miles of it. Then they would follow the shoreline of Grand Bahama Island to Freeport, which was their destination.

Fifteen minutes later, they were airborne. They flew over Lake Worth and the intercoastal waterway and were still climbing as the plane cleared the Florida coast leaving the palm trees and Australian pines of Palm Beach behind. Corner radioed back to West

Palm Beach tower that his plane, number N5-126K, was off Palm Beach en route to Freeport. But it never reached its Bahamian destination.

As soon as the FAA notified the coast guard of the missing plane, a search and rescue operation was put into motion. Navy, air force, Civil Air Patrol, and coast guard aircraft commenced searching. The cutters *Dauntless* and *Cape Fox* worked along the eastern edges of the Gulf Stream. The *Point Charles* and *Point Barnes* patrolled the western side of the Stream. The search covered an area extending from the Florida Keys to Portsmouth, Virginia, and 150 miles seaward. Winds were twelve knots with seas less than three feet. There were scattered heavy thunderstorms, but they were far enough apart for an airplane to fly around them.

On May 29, as dusk swept across the "Devil's Triangle," the search was terminated. No trace of the missing black-and-white airplane, Bob Corner, or Reno Rigon was found. Little or no mention of this incident was made in the south Florida newspapers, but the plane's vanishing is just as puzzling as the disappearances of the *Star Tiger, Star Ariel,* and the other airplanes in the "Devil's Triangle."

And there are still other planes vanishing at the rate of about one a month in the "triangle" that remain unreported. It is not that no one knows they have disappeared, but rather that those involved or associated with these "mystery aircraft" prefer to maintain a shroud of secrecy around their activities. These are the "pot pilots" and their "acid airliners" that are engaged in the lucrative business of smuggling hard drugs from Jamaica and Columbia into Florida. Because of the immense profits realized from the transportation and sale of these drugs, the heroin carriers place profits first, secrecy second, and safety last. The planes are dangerously overloaded as they head for some remote or deserted landing strip in south Florida. A number are known to have actually crashed on takeoff because they couldn't get airborne with their excessive weights. They carry only enough fuel to reach their Florida rendezvous point, unload, and proceed to a regular field where they clear customs as legitimate vacationers or businessmen returning from the West Indies. Others don't bother with customs because they never gave notice when they departed the United States. Thus, they are never missed when they disappear in their overloaded underfueled planes. If Herbie Pond, the first smuggler to vanish in the "triangle," knew of the conditions under which these dope runners fly, he would, no doubt, float up from his watery grave.

It was unusually cold in south Florida on Saturday, December 4, 1971. It was one of those rare times when ornate fireplaces became functional. A cold front was moving down from the north just as one had done almost twenty-six years previously when five navy planes took off from Fort Lauderdale Naval Air Station never to be seen again.

By 8 P.M., Robert N. Fischer and his wife Judy had put their three small daughters to bed in their home on the intercoastal waterway in Fort Lauderdale and were sitting in front of the color television set in the security of their family room watching Miami television station WPTV. Vincent Price was narrating a special about a mysterious sector of the North Atlantic called the "Devil's Triangle."

Later when discussing the show with friends who had also seen it, Dr. Fischer, a prominent bone surgeon, listened to a number of theories. A number of his patients also talked about the "Devil's Triangle" with him. They expressed their thoughts on the subject, but Fischer just listened. When they mentioned natural phenomena, he would nod in agreement. When the supernatural was suggested, the doctor merely listened without comment. It was only to a few close friends that the doctor voiced his own philosophy. His feeling was that the disappearances were the results of incidents that could be fully explained scientifically if all the facts were known. Little did he know that he would one day find out in person.

On the morning of Friday, August 10, 1973, the Fischers and their two younger daughters drove to the airport to begin their trip to Great Abaco Island in the Bahamas. The family planned to spend the weekend at Marsh Harbor and fly back to Fort Lauderdale on Sunday night, leaving their oldest daughter, twelve-year-old Laura, in Fort Lauderdale in order that she might participate in a tennis tournament. Fischer would pilot a plane borrowed from another Fort Lauderdale physician, Dr. Frank Stuart, who was vacationing aboard a yacht in Nassau.

At 10:46 A.M., the thirty-nine-year-old Fischer taxied the single-engine Beechcraft Bonanza away from Sunny South Flying Service at Fort Lauderdale—Hollywood International Airport. He had telephoned the FAA earlier stating that he would file a flight plan after takeoff, a commonly accepted procedure. When the plane reached the end of the runway alongside Interstate Highway I-95, Judy Fischer, thirty-eight, leaned back and double-checked the seat belts on seven-year-old Julie and three-year-old Melinda. A line of thunderstorms could be seen building up twenty-five to thirty miles to the east, although the weather was bright and sunny in Fort Lauderdale. The doctor checked the controls and instruments.

Then as he moved the throttle, the engine revved up and the plane began to move. A big Eastern Airlines jet roared down the runway bound for New York. The yellow-and-green Beechcraft moved up to the runway. Fischer radioed the tower, "7956 KILO ready to go."

"7956 KILO, clear for takeoff," replied the tower. Fischer opened the throttle, and the plane sped down the field and became airborne. Once he reached cruising altitude, Fischer headed east out over the Atlantic. The flight to Abaco was to take two and one-half hours. The plane had a four- to five-hour fuel supply. Fischer either forgot or was unable to file his flight plan after becoming airborne, for the last words ever heard from him were, "7956 KILO ready to go."

A number of other planes that attempted to fly to the Bahamas that day turned back because of weather and radio interference. Several reported that they returned because they were unable to establish radio contact to file a flight plan with the tower while still in sight of land. Did Dr. Fischer, while unable to make radio contact, keep going, and when he found his plane hopelessly trapped in a thunderstorm become completely disoriented? Or did something else happen out there?

At 8:20 P.M. Miami coast guard was notified that the Fischers' plane had not arrived at Marsh Harbor. Darkness delayed an air search but the 210-foot cutter *Dauntless*, which was standing by in Miami Beach on two-hour search and rescue service notice, prepared to get under way. She would be on station off the Bahamas with her helicopter by the first light of dawn.

At daybreak five coast guard aircraft accompanied by one navy and one air force plane were winging their way to their respective search areas. After steaming all night at eighteen knots, the *Dauntless* was already searching the area off Grand Bahama Island and her helicopter was launched and searching to the south. Civil Air Patrol planes were searching over the Florida Everglades.

By Saturday afternoon, seven civilian planes, all manned by friends of the Fischers, joined the search, working grid areas assigned to them by the coast guard. As darkness fell, twelve of the fourteen aircraft returned to their bases. Two, the helicopter from the *Dauntless* and a coast guard Albatross amphibian, worked far into the night using powerful lights called "midnight sunlamps." Nothing was found.

The search was resumed on Sunday. In addition to military aircraft, there were three airplanes from the Bahama Air-Sea Rescue Service and ten private planes searching for some trace of the Fischers and their two little girls. Some areas, along the missing plane's intended route, were scoured again and again in hopes of finding some signs of survivors or debris. "It doesn't really look too good," said Lieutenant John Brooks, the duty officer at the Miami Beach Coast Guard Base, Sunday night. "When we have an aircraft missing, we usually search three to five days. If we don't find them in the first couple of days, or on the third day, chances get kind of slim.

"Survival in cases like this just depends on the strength of the individuals involved and how long they are willing to fight to stay alive," Brooks continued. "If the family is able to cling to the debris from the aircraft, keep themselves from drinking any saltwater, and not give up hope, their chances are better. Rainfall, also, could help by providing them with fresh drinking water."

Shortly before noon on Monday, the helicopter from the *Dauntless* recovered an open, but uninflated, life raft from the water twenty-five miles southwest of the Bahamian resort city of Freeport. A check of the serial number stenciled on the bright yellow raft revealed that it was one of two sold by the manufacturer to the B'hia Mar marine store in Fort Lauderdale. Both had been resold by the store, one to Dr. Frank Stuart, the missing plane's owner. The purchaser of the other raft was unknown and an exhaustive, but fruitless, effort was made to locate him. Although remote, the possibility existed that there might be another plane or a boat lost out there.

Tuesday night the coast guard called off the search with the following statement: "It's probably futile to continue the search. The search is suspended pending further development. If there is any indication that the family might still be alive, the search will be resumed."

Harry Vordermeier, Jr., his brother Ken, Walter McCrory, Ken Whittington, Dr. Nile Lestrange, and several other friends of the Fischers who had been searching in their own planes gathered in front of a hangar that evening and decided to continue searching on their own at least through the following weekend. The days came and went, and each day it was the same story—nothing.

On the last day of the extended search, Harry Vordermeier had a hunch. He decided to fly along the shoreline of Little Abaco Island on the possibility that the life raft wasn't from the Fischers' plane and that they might have made it that far. Flying along the island's desolate south shore, he spotted something silvery in the brush. It looked like part of an airplane. Walter McCrory, accompanied by Mrs. Fischer's brother, rented a jeep and proceeded to the remote area of the sighting. It was definitely aircraft wreckage, but not from the Fischers' plane. It had been exposed to the elements for many months. Whose airplane could the wreckage have come from? The styrofoam-backed aluminum could not have come from any aircraft reported missing in recent years. It did not match any of the lost planes. There were no markings or other identification clues as to where it came from or who was flying it.

Once again, while looking for one victim, searchers discovered evidence of another, but one whose disappearance had not been reported. The "Devil's Triangle" in giving up one of its secrets had disclosed only enough to tell us that more is happening out there than we know.

4. Voyages to Nowhere

As the treasure-laden galleon entered the channel between Serranilla and Pedro Shoals, furious winds burst down upon her, winds that signaled but one meaning—hurricane. The *Genovese* was swept eastward before driving seas. Her crew, those not washed overboard, struggled desperately to cut loose the twisted snarl of torn rigging and smashed spars. All the sails were gone, either ripped to shreds or blown away by the shrieking wind. Yet her hull moved faster through the water than it ever had under full sail. With an almost predictable regularity the wind or sea would indiscriminately carry some poor soul into the raging waters. Men fought each other to man the pumps. The pump handles were all that was left on deck to hold onto. Their faces were bleeding from the sting of the gale-driven salt spume. Those who dared to open their eyes into the wind were instantly blinded. The inevitable end came. Not suddenly, but slowly—that is if anything can be slow in a hurricane. The *Genovese*'s bottom scraped over the outer edges of Banner Reef. Bottom planking began to shred. At first a plank forward. Then one aft. The pumps became useless. The anchor was dropped. A half-dozen men were carried over the side with it. Tons of gold and silver poured onto the ocean floor through the ever-increasing number of holes in the hull. A king's ransom had been scattered over miles of ocean floor. When the galleon finally crashed high upon a coral reef, only a handful of the crew managed to survive. They clung to the wrecked hulk until the winds and seas abated and rescuers found them. The date was August 23, 1730.

The loss of the *Genovese* was one of the first recorded shipwrecks on the Pedro Bank, which lies about fifty miles south of the western tip of Jamaica. Down through the years, more than a score of vessels have fallen victim to those treacherous shallows.

Almost every account of the "Devil's Triangle" has included mention of the sixty-three-foot *Sno' Boy* out of Kingston, Jamaica, that vanished near the Pedro Bank with between thirty-five and fifty-seven fishermen and crew. The *Sno' Boy* has seldom been given more than a sentence or two. The writers merely state that she disappeared in the "triangle" while en route from Kingston to Northeast Cay with forty persons aboard. There is no mention of the treacherous currents and coral heads abounding in the area of Northeast Cay or of the weather.

The vessel left Kingston on Tuesday, July 2, 1963. Her captain was Louis Tole. It has never been established exactly how many were aboard as she headed for Northeast Cay, which is a spit of an island in the northeast part of the perfidious Pedro Bank. The *Sno' Boy* was a converted ASR (Air-Sea Rescue) boat of the type used to rescue downed aviators and imperiled seamen before helicopters were adopted to that purpose. With their original twin engines, either

Packards or Hall-Scotts, the ASRs had a capability exceeding forty knots burning forty gallons of fuel per hour in each engine during the process. Those who bought them surplus from the government, such as Robert Braman of Miami, owner of the *Sno' Boy*, usually replaced the high-speed gas engines with slower, more economical diesels. The hulls were constructed of a double layer of diagonal planking to withstand hours of pounding through rolling seas. Their profile was similar to the larger PT boats. In fact, so much did they resemble each other that most of the "PT boats" in the movie *PT-109* were disguised ASRs. Braman had leased the vessel to Byron Hill of Kingston, who in cooperation with the Jamaican government, was using it to promote that country's fishing industry.

On July 4, the *Sno' Boy* was reported as missing with fifty-five persons aboard. On the following day the navy reported her as being safe. She had sought refuge in a small harbor due to bad weather.

Two days later the Associated Press reported the vessel as still missing. The erroneous announcement that she had been located resulted from a similar ASR boat belonging to the Colombian Navy having taken refuge in that small harbor.

Ten planes from the aircraft carrier *Wasp* had joined the search along with a number of surface vessels. It was still unknown how many persons had been aboard the missing boat for the eighty-mile trip to the Pedro Bank. On July 6, the harbor master at Kingston reported that a fishing vessel, the *Marsotana*, had found what could have been a tabletop from the *Sno' Boy* two and one-half miles northeast of Northeast Cay.

On July 7, the destroyer *Malloy* reported that it was picking up debris including sections of diagonal planking, parts of a wheel house, life jackets, paneling, and a body in a fifteen-square-mile area fifty miles south of Jamaica. A coast guard spokesman stated that from the evidence recovered, the *Sno' Boy* was either swamped by high seas or broke up on a reef. From the condition of the salvaged items, all indications seem to point to the latter. Thus, one more "unsolved" mystery of the "Devil's Triangle" can be considered as never having really been a strange disappearance at all. It was simply a matter of the twenty-five-thousand-dollar vessel being overloaded to the extent that she was unmanageable when caught in a storm near the reefs of Pedro Bank. She was crowded with fishermen, carrying nineteen tons of ice, drums of water and gasoline, food and supplies, and bundles of bamboo poles. Her dinghy and life raft were later found, but there was no indication that they had ever been occupied. The only mystery about the *Sno' Boy* is how many men did she carry to a watery grave—thirty-six, forty, fifty-five, fifty-seven?

The *Sno' Boy*, too, had joined the *Genovese* in one of the Caribbean's numerous graveyards of lost ships, but she didn't disappear in the "Devil's Triangle."

On March 15, 1910, the navy tug, U.S.S. *Nina*, departed Norfolk Navy Yard. She was bound for Havana, Cuba, where she was to serve as one of the support ships during the salvage operation of the battleship *Maine*. The tug was seen off Savannah, Georgia, steaming south. She was never seen or heard from again. She was the first steam-powered navy vessel to disappear in the "Devil's Triangle."

The chronicles of the United States Navy abound with stories of famous ships, ships such as the *Constitution, Constellation, Wasp, Hornet, Bonhomme*

Richard, Essex, Enterprise, Monitor, Maine, Arizona, Yorktown, and *Missouri.* For every ship that has achieved fame and glory, there are dozens that have been lost in the pages of history. The U.S.S. *Grampus* is one of those unremembered ships.

On May 1, 1822, the *Grampus,* under the command of Lieutenant H. Gregory, captured four pirate schooners off Sugar Key in the Straits of Florida. On May 12, she captured two more. Then on August 16, after an all day running gun battle, she captured the pirate schooner *Palmyra.*

The *Grampus* captured two pirate vessels on May 22, of the following year. The pirates had double the firepower of the naval vessel. This action occurred off Campeche, Mexico.

On March 3, 1825, the *Grampus,* after a three-day chase along the south coast of Puerto Rico, caught a pirate sloop that had been playing havoc with merchant vessels for over a year. This confrontation was one of the last engagements between ships of the United States Navy and the few remaining pirate vessels. Ships such as the *Grampus* had driven the skull and crossbones out of the West Indies once and for all.

For the next five years the *Grampus* patrolled the waters of the Caribbean and Gulf of Mexico looking after American interests. Then on June 5, 1830, while working her way through the Windward Passage, her lookout spied a suspicious sail off Cape Haitien, Haiti. Closer investigation revealed that it was the bark *Fenix,* long suspected, but never proved, to be a slave ship. The *Grampus* took chase and soon overtook the *Fenix.* A boarding party discovered the bark to be a slaver. Her holds were crammed with Africans. Thus, the *Grampus* saved over three hundred blacks from a life of servitude. Word spread among vessels plying the Caribbean in illicit trades to steer clear of the *Grampus*.

In 1836, she was assigned to support land forces during the Seminole Indian campaign in Florida. On August 25, the *Grampus* landed a detachment of marines in Tampa Bay to protect settlers from marauding Indians. She supported American land forces in Florida until the Indian campaign officially ended on August 14, 1842.

The *Grampus* patrolled West Indian waters through March 1, 1843. On that date after twenty-one years of yeoman service in Florida and Caribbean waters, she was finally ordered home to Charleston. She was sighted homeward bound by the *Madison* off Saint Augustine, Florida, on March 3. She was never seen again. The *Grampus*, the heroic ship that became lost in the pages of history, also became lost in that body of water that would one day be referred to as the "Devil's Triangle."

On Friday, October 9, 1971, the longshoremen at Barranquilla, Colombia, finished a week's loading of the 338-foot motor ship *Caribe*. The cargo was bulk cement. The vessel's owners, Dominican-Bordas Lines, had contracted to deliver the cargo to Santo Domingo, Dominican Republic, some seven hundred miles to the east north east. The next morning the bulk carrier with its twenty-eight-man crew sailed ten miles down the Magdalena River and out into the Caribbean.

On Sunday night the ship contacted the owners informing them that the ship would be arriving at its destination on Tuesday. That was the last that was ever heard of the *Caribe*. Although she was plying through heavily traveled shipping lanes that she had sailed many times in the past, she was never seen again. She carried an up-to-date communications system, yet no distress signal was ever transmitted. A joint search effort by coast guard and navy planes of the United States, Colombia, and the Dominican Republic failed to find any evidence whatsoever.

A number of theories were brought forth varying from Colombian guerrillas hijacking the *Caribe* to Cuba to an explosion from superfine cement dust that remained suspended in the air spaces in the upper part of the vessel's holds. But these theories along with others were discounted as being too remote. The ship was simply listed as "lost at sea, cause unknown." It was a familiar story—no survivors, no victims, no wreckage.

It is often said that the days of "wooden ships and iron men" are gone forever. This is an erroneous statement, for the United States Navy still maintains a fleet of wooden ships. One could even refer to their crews as iron men at times. Although these vessels are but 165-feet long and displace less than six hundred tons, they work in the open seas in all weather. They are the navy's minesweepers. As long as magnetic mines are used in warfare at sea, the navies of the world will utilize these wooden vessels.

Typical of these ocean minesweepers is the U.S.S. *Sturdy*. Her four Packard diesels propel her at fifteen and one-half knots. All of her metal fittings are stainless steel, bronze, or some other nonmagnetic material. Her crew consists of seventy-five officers and men.

The July 14, 1968, issue of the Fort Lauderdale *News* ran a feature story about the "Devil's Triangle." It was headlined, "Fifty-Three Area Persons Lost in 'Triangle' in Last Twenty-Five Years."

On the following day, July 15, the same newspaper ran a story about one of the most mysterious incidents to have occurred in the "triangle." The *Sturdy* was returning from training maneuvers 150 miles east of Jacksonville, Florida, when one of her lookouts spotted an object floating ahead off the port bow. The captain ordered the course changed and headed his vessel in the direction of the sighting. As the vessel pulled alongside the object, the crew discovered that they had found the waterlogged hulk of a yacht or fishing vessel. After scraping off some of the marine growth, they were able to make out *Crystal* and Fort George Island, Florida. They radioed the coast guard in Jacksonville of their find. A short while later the coast guard radioed back that it had no record or report of such a vessel missing or overdue.

Several hours later a second message was received from the coast guard by the *Sturdy*. The context of the transmission was that there was, indeed, a vessel named the *Crystal* from Fort George Island, Florida, missing with all aboard it. However, the coast guard had terminated the search and given the *Crystal* up for lost four years earlier in 1964.

On April 3, less than two months after the huge ocean liner *Queen Elizabeth I*, re-named *Seawise University*, departed Port Everglades on her last voyage, a trouble-plagued journey that ended with her destruction by a mysterious fire in Hong Kong Harbor, another black-hulled vessel, also named *Elizabeth*, voyaged forth from Port Everglades. But her departure went unheralded. The only ones to see her off were the few longshoremen handling the dock lines and the ship's agent. She had just completed taking aboard two thousand tons of baled wastepaper bound for recycling in Venezuela. The 191-foot converted navy landing ship, renamed *Elizabeth*, was owned by the Orinoco Shipping Company of Paterson, New Jersey.

The *Elizabeth* was a fairly fast vessel for her age and size. Two days later on April 5, the owners received a message that she was clearing the Bahamas and entering the Windward Passage, that body of water separating Haiti and Cuba. That was the last message ever received from the *Elizabeth*. On May 1, the coast guard in Miami received a telegram from the owners that their vessel was overdue in Venezuela. A search conducted from the Bahama Islands through the West Indies and all the way to Venezuela turned up no trace of the missing ship.

Speculation was that the old and tired wartime vessel broke up and sank. But her cargo was bales of compressed paper, and bales of compressed wastepaper can float for days. A rolled-up newspaper can float for hours. If the *Elizabeth* did break up, the area should have been swarming with bales of floating paper—bales that should have been spotted by other vessels or planes, for the ill-fated ship had been traveling along the busiest shipping lane between the United States, Central America, and northern South America.

According to maritime tradition it is bad luck to change a vessel's name. Could this have influenced the fate of the two black-hulled vessels named *Elizabeth*, one a queen and one a tramp, that put to sea from Port Everglades and entered the "Devil's Triangle" within sixty days of each other in 1971? Exactly thirty years before the *Queen Elizabeth* had her name changed, another ship had her name changed and sailed off into the "Devil's Triangle."

At 9:09 A.M. on Wednesday, March 12, 1941, from a point somewhere six hundred miles east of Jacksonville, Florida, echoed an SOS: "Lowering boats . . . crew abandoning ship." The vessel was identified as the *Mahukona*, which had departed Norfolk two days earlier with thirty-two hundred tons of coal bound for Rio de Janiero. Four vessels in the immediate area changed course and sped toward the stricken ship. They were the coast guard cutters *Bibb* and *Modoc*, the freighter *West Shipper*, and the Puerto Rico bound liner *Borinquen*. The latter was the first to arrive at the last position given by the *Mahukona*. No wreckage was sighted nor could any survivors be found.

The *Mahukona* was built in 1919 by the Great Lakes Ship Building Corporation for the Matson Navigation Company. She had seen all of her service in the Pacific. She was laid up in storage from 1928 until 1940, when she was refitted at a cost of seventy-five thousand dollars and moved to the East Coast for delivery to France. However, upon the surrender of France to the Germans, the Maritime Commission canceled the sale. She was then sold to Navebras, Inc., a Brazilian company, and renamed the *Santa Clara*.

On March 16, the cutter *Bibb* reported finding wreckage near Bermuda that appeared to be from the *Mahukona*. The debris included part of a deck house, a section of mast, and two life jackets—one with the name *Mahukona* and one with that name freshly painted over and the name *Santa Clara* painted in. No trace of life boats or any of the twenty-six crew members was ever found. Could the ship have succumbed to the so-called curse of the "Devil's Triangle," or could it have been the old sailors' legend of the sea?

During the period from 1920 to 1933, when the Eighteenth Amendment of the United States prohibited the use, manufacture, transfer, sale, importation, and exportation of intoxicating liquors, there was born a new breed of adventurer—the rumrunner.

These men did not attain the notoriety of the boot-leggers or the infamy of the hijackers. One might have classified them as blockade runners, because they were constantly evading the patrolling vessels of the United States Revenue Service and coast guard. Most of the hijackers are dead. The bootleggers have no desire to remember. But those still living who ran the illicit booze into this country by boat or aircraft during the Prohibition era still show a twinkle in their eyes when reminiscing about "the old days." They were a swashbuckling group.

Miami-built boats were considered the ultimate craft for rum-running. In fact, some of the boats designed specifically for the purpose of making a quick dash across the Gulf Stream from the Bahamas to Florida are the models for today's cruising and sports fishing boats.

Hundreds of these boats ran the gauntlet from the West Indies to the mainland. Four or five successful trips could pay for one's boat. After that, it was all profit. But it was easier said than done. Many were successful, some were apprehended by the coast guard or revenue agents, and others disappeared under puzzling circumstances. A number of things might have happened to this latter group. They could have been gunned down by hijackers and their boats and bodies sent to the bottom. Or a boatman might have accepted a large sum of money from a bootlegger with which to purchase contraband whiskey and simply absconded. Or he might have bought the booze and sold it to another bootlegger before absconding. Then, too, they were all operating well within the confines of the "Devil's Triangle."

Many states have had to cope with vicious outlaw gangs. Eventually these gunmen become eulogized into legendary folklore heroes. There were the James brothers of Missouri, the Doolins of Oklahoma, the Daltons, and others such as Florida's Ashley gang. In the period after World War I, the four Ashley brothers, led by John, left their imprint on Florida's history with a trail of bank robberies and shootings up and down the peninsula. John was eventually captured. Bob Ashley was killed trying to free John after killing two deputies.

The other two brothers, Ed and Frank, moonlighted from their bank robberies by running rum from the Bahamas to Florida. Their boat was one of the fastest. It should have been, because the banks paid for it.

One evening in March, 1924, when the Gulf Stream was quite smooth except for an occasional rain shower, Ed and Frank set off from Grand Bahama Island for the fifty-mile run to Palm Beach with a boatload of whiskey. However, they never reached the mainland. They had vanished. The weather had been good, and the usually reliable underworld "grapevine" gave no indication of the two brothers having been hijacked.

During this period, John Ashley was serving time at the Florida State Prison at Raiford. The news of his brothers' disappearance struck him deeply. One night several weeks later, John had a dream that a rival gang had killed his brothers after hijacking their eighteen-thousand-dollar load of bootleg whiskey. In May, John Ashley escaped from prison.

A month later the three members of the rival gang, Beau Stokes, Dick Allen, and Ed White took off in their high-speed boat from Palm Beach heading for West End in the Bahamas. Somewhere in the fifty-mile stretch of water separating Palm Beach from West End the three men disappeared, because they never arrived at their destination to pick up the load of liquor waiting for them. They were never seen again. Whether they had killed the two Ashley brothers and whether John Ashley killed them because of a dream will forever remain a mystery. What bank guards, police, revenuers, and sheriffs' posses couldn't do, the "Devil's Triangle" did.

The history of Japanese seafaring is abound with legends of sea monsters, demons, and ghost ships. But the seas of Japan are a great distance from the waters of the "Devil's Triangle." The crew of the freighter *Raifuku Maru* no doubt congratulated themselves when they signed on in January, 1921, for a voyage that would take them from the frigid waters of their homeland to the warm waters of the Caribbean and tropical Atlantic—and presumably on to New York.

The *Raifuku Maru* made an uneventful passage across the Pacific, through the Panama Canal, and into the Caribbean. But as the ship steamed past the Bahama Islands, the Japanese crew found that strange happenings were more than legend in the waters of the western Atlantic, for the last that was ever heard from the freighter *Raifuku Maru* was the code message: "Danger like dagger now. Come quick!" Then silence.

What had happened to the Japanese ship? During the first half of 1921, at least ten other large ships disappeared in the western Atlantic. No less than six sailed from Newport News alone never to be heard from again. There was some speculation of mass piracy. But had the *Raifuku Maru* been attacked by pirates, just the word "pirates" would have been a faster and simpler message to transmit. A UFO? UFOlogists have described saucer-, oval-, and cigar-shaped objects—but never one resembling a dagger.

One possibility that is more feasible than any other explanation is a waterspout—a tornado at sea. There are differences of opinions among meteorologists as to the destructive force of a waterspout. To watch one is an eerie experience. But to be aboard a vessel that is being struck by one is an experience almost beyond description.

Imagine yourself voyaging through subtropical seas aboard a small tramp ship. The holds are crammed with concrete blocks, steel beams, and sacks of cement. The deck cargo is tiers of lumber secured by chains made taut with chain tighteners and turnbuckles. The cargo is destined for a tourist complex being constructed on a private West Indian island.

For the past two days sea conditions have been ideal. Eight- to ten-knot head winds have made sitting under the awning aft of the wheelhouse most relaxing. But now that cooling wind is no more. The ship's wake creates the only blemish on the mirrorlike surface of the sea. Her speed of six knots barely creates a feeling of air movement.

Ahead to the southeast a line of gray clouds have formed. Soon the clouds have massed into one. Their gray color is darkening. The upper layers appear to be reaching into the stratosphere where they are spreading out into an anvil shape. The lower fringe is almost straight except for occasional saw-toothed edges. In a matter of minutes one of the fang-shaped jagged edges slowly extends down toward the surface of the sea. The ship is moving closer. Lower and lower the fang reaches. It no longer resembles a fang. It now looks more like the blade of a dagger. Almost to the water . . . it stops. The ship still moves closer. Another dagger is rising up out of the sea toward the first one. They merge into a single mass. It now moves across the water. The phenomenal happening has so awed you that only now you realize the captain must turn the ship as the freighter is on a collision course with the gray black funnel-shaped mass.

Although he is not a mulatto, the skipper's features indicate that somewhere along his black lineage was a white ancestor. His perpetual uniform consists of rubber-thong sandles, knee-length beltless khaki shorts that seem to defy gravity unless they are held up by the huge wrinkle under his potbelly, and a battered officer's cap with the word *Captain* in gold braid above the visor. The cap must have survived numerous storms, voyages, barroom brawls, and other captains. The Honduran master impresses you as being a bundle of seagoing joviality. But within this fat-faced little man is a streak of stubbornness.

The ship maintains its course. So does the tornado of the sea. A confrontation between man and nature is inevitable. The spectral phenomenon and the ship converge. The steady rhythm of the ancient diesel is drowned out by the roar of the tornado. Except for the captain and the helmsman, you are the only one still topside. The crew has fled below. The man at the wheel tightens his grip on the spokes as you move into the wheelhouse. The captain remains out on the flying bridge. The roar has become the sound of an express train bearing down on you. No, it's the sound of a dozen express trains. Visibility is gone. It is as though the ship has sailed right under the cataract of Niagara Falls. Something is happening out on deck. You can't tell what.

In less than a half minute the deluge is gone and the sea is back to normal, but not the ship. The lumber that was on deck is now in the sea, leaving an expanding trail across the ocean as the victor of the confrontation moves off. A number of hatch covers too are gone. The vessel's railings are a twisted mass of metal. The thousand-pound steel booms have been lifted out of their cradles and dropped onto the deck. The captain, bloodied and naked, is sitting on deck, his arms and legs wrapped around a stanchion. Still smiling, he comments on how fresh the water tasted. The rest of that day and the following day are spent recovering lumber and cargo hatches from the sea. You have been through a water spout.*

Like the sea itself, waterspouts are unpredictable. There have been incidents of ships coming in contact with them and surviving unscathed. On other occasions vessels have been known to succumb to these seagoing tornados. Theodolite measurements document evidence of waterspouts having attained heights in excess of eight thousand feet with shafts measuring fifteen hundred feet across. Could the Japanese crew of the *Raifuku Maru*, never having seen a waterspout before, conceive the vortex of one, because of panic or language barrier, as "like dagger"?

Just as the Christmas season seems to be a bad time for aircraft, small boats, and yachts in the "Triangle," February and March appear to be the most hazardous months for large ships. Lost during either a February or a March were the *Marine Sulphur Queen*, the *Cyclops*, the *Mahukona*, the *Raifuku Maru*, the *Carroll A. Deering*, and the *Hewitt* to name just a few.

On March 13, 1926, the freighter *Suduffco* sailed from Port Newark, New Jersey—in spite of the old sailors' superstition that it is bad luck to start a voyage on the thirteenth. Her cargo consisted of four thousand tons of steel pipe valued at five hundred thousand dollars. She was bound for Panama and

*From an actual experience of the author.

scheduled to arrive on March 22. Her captain had over twenty-five years of experience at sea. On April 7, her owners reported the ship overdue. A search that lasted two weeks turned up nothing to reveal her fate. The *Suduffco* and her crew of twenty-eight were never heard from again. Another vessel had fallen victim to the "triangle" during the February-March months.

In 1921, a record number of ships vanished during the first three months of that year. The list reads almost like a U-boat commander's war diary—the Italian steamer *Monte San Michele*, the British steamer *Esperanza de Larrinaga*, the Brazilian steamer *Cabedello*, the British tanker *Ottawa* (the above vessels all cleared port on February 2 and 3), the sulphur ship *Hewitt*, and three Norwegian barks, the *Steinsund*, the *Florino*, and the *Svartskog*. No trace whatsoever was found of any of these eight ships. Several months previous to these disappearances, two other vessels put to sea never to be seen again. They were the Russian bark *Albyan*, which sailed on October 1, 1920, and the Spanish steamer *Yute* that cleared port on November 14, 1920. Every one of these ships had departed from a port on the East Coast of the United States. Some had entered the "triangle." Others had skirted around to the north of the area. There is no knowledge at all of the fate of these ships.

A safe conjecture as to what befell some of the doomed vessels would result from the winter of 1920–21 being one of the worst on record in the North Atlantic. At times the winds exceeded hurricane force, including during the first and second weeks of February, 1921. Hurricane force winds in the tropics are dangerous for any vessel, but winds in excess of seventy-five miles per hour blowing down out of the Arctic can be sheer hell. Ships would become coated

with ice faster than the crews could chop it away.
Eventually the superstructures and masts would be
so covered with ice that the vessels would become
dangerously top-heavy. The huge seas accompanying
the winds could easily capsize any such top-heavy
ships were they to broach and be caught broadside in
a trough between two waves. Useless lifeboats frozen
in their chocks would have plummeted to the bottom
with the ships. Life rafts that would have normally
broken free from a capsized ship would have had
their release levers frozen. Any possible survivors
would last but a few short minutes under such conditions. The waters of the North Atlantic would have
become as terrible as those off Cape Horn.

According to the U.S. Weather Bureau, winds up
to ninety knots swept a one-thousand-mile-long section of the Atlantic shipping lanes for three days beginning February 6. Again on February 15, terrible
storms arose in mid-Atlantic and raged for seventy-
two hours. The bureau's files contain reports from
a number of ships that passed through those February
storms and reached port only after having sustained a
considerable amount of damage. There were no accounts of anything strange except the weather. Yet,
never before or since have so many ships disappeared
in a small sector of the Atlantic Ocean in such a
short span of time.

More than a few vessels that have vanished in
the "Devil's Triangle" do have a touch of the bizarre
associated with their disappearances. The sixty-five-
foot schooner *Home Sweet Home* out of Philadelphia
was bound for a winter in the Caribbean early in
January, 1955. After laying over for several days in
Bermuda, the schooner set sail for Antigua some twelve
hundred miles across an open body of water some-

times referred to as the Sargasso Sea. The date was January 13, 1955. Apparently none of the seven persons aboard were superstitious about sailing on the thirteenth. It was 5 A.M. when the ship put out to sea. Aboard were the owner Ward Wheelock, a Philadelphia advertising executive; his wife; their son Ian; Kent Willing, senior trust officer of the Girard Trust Corn Exchange Bank of Philadelphia; his wife; Harry Darrel of Bermuda, the boat's captain; and crewman Miller Powell, also of Bermuda.

Gales fierce enough to cause a number of ships to send out distress messages swept down on the area later that day. On January 27, the *Home Sweet Home* was reported overdue at Antigua, and a search began. An air force B-29 spotted an unusual-looking unidentifiable object floating 605 miles southeast of Bermuda during the search. The coast guard cutter *Duane* heard the plane's report and asked for a position. The pilot radioed that the plane was encountering difficulties with its navigation equipment and could not give an exact location. The pilot also stated that the unidentified object was definitely not part of the missing yacht. The cutter, which was already carrying eight survivors from a downed C-54, proceeded to the approximate area but could find no trace of the unidentifiable object seen floating on the water nor was the *Home Sweet Home* found.

Ten years before the *Home Sweet Home* was listed as missing, two other large schooners were the subject of a search. On December 27, 1945, just after all hope for the six navy planes lost off Florida had been given up, the *New York Times* reported two large schooners missing. One was the seventy-foot *Voyager II* being taken down the intercoastal waterway by retired army officer Gifford Hitz, Jr., of Westport,

Connecticut, and his three teen-aged children. No checkpoints along the waterway reported seeing the vessel.

In the same paper was a story about the two-masted schooner *Valmore* and a crew of four. The two-master was being towed by the *Dunworkin* out of Morehead City, North Carolina. The towing craft became disabled and cut the schooner free. The *Dunworkin* eventually drifted ashore and was wrecked on the beach. But the *Valmore* and her four-man crew have not been seen since.

It was a chilly Friday afternoon for Florida on January 14, 1949, when Captain Johnny Pellet pulled his thirty-six-foot cabin cruiser *Driftwood* up to Dink Frost's dock for fuel, bait, and other supplies. Dink Frost sold bait and fuel to most boats from Dania, which is the next city to the south of Fort Lauderdale. Aboard the *Driftwood* with Pellet were Bert LaBree, a Dania insurance and real estate broker; Dania City building inspector Paul J. Heckert; Logan Eisle, a Nashville, Tennessee, industrialist; and Dr. Albert Sullivan, a physician from Nashville. The five men were starting out on a five-day fishing trip near Bimini in the Bahamas.

After fueling and taking aboard the bait and supplies, Pellet cast off and pointed the *Driftwood's* bow to the southeast as the boat cleared the inlet at Port Everglades. The party anticipated arriving at Bimini the next morning. They would fish for four days and start back for Dania on Tuesday night, arriving home Wednesday morning. The boat had just come out of the boatyard where the bottom was painted and the twin Chrysler engines were overhauled. It was in excellent condition. Johnny Pellet had made the crossing to the Bahamas nearly a hundred times.

Although the night became chilly, it was still good cruising weather. As the sun receded toward the horizon, the Gulf Stream's azure blue water made its usual transitory change to dark blue, darker blue, and finally to black. Once away from land, most sailors find dusk on the ocean a time of solitude. Even a moonless night does not have the folornness of dusk at sea. Maybe it is the time passage from the light of day to the black of night and the feeling that the darkness could bring the unexpected. The *Driftwood* motored on into the night.

Dink Frost wasn't too concerned when the *Driftwood* failed to return on Wednesday morning as scheduled. He figured fishing must have been good and the men decided to spend an extra day at Bimini.

On the following morning as Frost sat drinking his coffee, he read in the paper about a massive air and sea search. The navy, coast guard, and air force were conducting the operation in quest of a British South American Airways airliner that had disappeared between Bermuda and Jamaica with twenty-four persons aboard.

Frost set the paper down atop a brand-new ship-to-shore radio belonging to Johnny Pellet. Pellet had planned to install the radio in the *Driftwood* after the trip to Bimini. Frost telephoned a pilot friend who was flying a charter to Bimini later that morning. The pilot agreed to check with Pellet to see when the *Driftwood* would be returning.

Shortly after lunch Dink Frost received a message from the pilot in Bimini. The message was brief and short. The *Driftwood* had never arrived at Bimini, and no one had seen it around the islands. The coast guard was contacted immediately. Within the hour a second search was being conducted in the "Devil's Triangle." The searchers combed the Florida Strait as far north as Brunswick, Georgia. They searched eastward through the Bahamas and out into the open Atlantic until their search pattern overlapped that of those hunting the missing airliner. At the end of two weeks both search operations terminated. No traces of the yacht *Driftwood* or the airliner *Star Ariel* were ever found. Twenty-nine more names were added to the "triangle's" enigmatic roll.

In June, 1950, the freighter *Sandra* was loaded to her Plimsoll mark with a cargo of 350 tons of insecticide destined for Puerto Cabello, Venezuela. With her diesels propelling her at ten knots, she left the port of Savannah, Georgia, behind and headed south toward the Straits of Florida. Vessels making a southbound passage through the straits usually keep close to the Florida coastline in order to avoid the push of the Gulf Stream's north-flowing current. The stream's velocity is considerably less along its outer edges. If not in the sight of land, the vessels heading south are at least close enough to the coast to see the glow of lights from the various oceanfront cities. Any radio-equipped vessel taking this route is rarely more than an hour's flying time from a military air base should she get in trouble.

The *Sandra* was one of those vessels that got into trouble. But she never transmitted a distress call. Somewhere in the Straits of Florida between Jacksonville and Miami along one of the East Coast's busiest shipping lanes the 356-foot *Sandra* vanished from the face of the earth—or should we say from the face of the sea?

On October 27, 1969, Miami coast guard received a single distress call from a boat named either the *Keela* or *Tequila* stating that it was rapidly sinking in Florida Bay, that large area of shallow water separating the Florida Keys from the Gulf of Mexico. Aboard were three persons—a man, woman, and a child. They reported that their position was unknown as their compass and charts were lost overboard, but they thought that they were north of Islamarada. A search revealed no trace of a boat or any survivors in the area. Nor was there any report of such a boat or any man, woman, and child missing.

Sometimes a boat will send in a call for assistance, but will manage to remedy the problem and make it back to port under its own power and neglect to notify the authorities. Did this happen? Or was there never a family of three in trouble? Was the distress call one of the cruel prank signals received by the coast guard from time to time? Nevertheless, a distress call mandates a full search and rescue operation. Thus, while the boaters or pranksters are safe at home watching television or sleeping soundly in their beds, searchers are out at sea risking their lives looking for a vessel that is not missing.

If one hundred readers whose favorite subject is the sea were asked what was the greatest toll of life in any single maritime tragedy, ninety of them would invariably declare that it was the loss of the *Titanic* and 1,517 lives in the North Atlantic during her maiden voyage on April 15, 1912. But they would be wrong. Almost four years later the French auxiliary cruiser *Provence* went down in the Mediterranean on February 26, 1916, with a loss of no less than three thousand lives.

Of the same one hundred readers of the sea, ninety-nine would agree that the greatest single disaster in the "Devil's Triangle" was the loss of U.S.S. *Cyclops* en route from Barbados to Baltimore in 1918. In this disaster, 308 lives were lost. But again, they would be wrong.

On March 1, 1854, the black-hulled *City of Glasgow* was one of thirteen ships to sail from Liverpool bound for America. She carried 480 crew and passengers. Most of the latter were emigrating to the United States. The owners, the Liverpool and Philadelphia Steamship Company, claimed that their iron ship would make it to Philadelphia equally fast whether under sail or with her auxiliary steam engine.

By the second week in April, the 1,080-ton *City of Glasgow* should have entered Delaware Bay. But she hadn't. The owner's agents, Richardson Brothers and Company, suggested that her engine had broken down and that she was under sail in light airs. But April passed and still there was no word of the big ship.

During May, a number of rumors were reported in the newspapers: the *City of Glasgow* was locked in ice; she had been captured by pirates; the ship had foundered off the coast of Africa where all aboard were marooned on an isolated beach; and she had been seen near the Bahamas.

The last rumor might have a grain of truth in it. During March the ship's master would have sailed a course to take the vessel south of any areas where there was danger of ice flows. Also, the farther south he sailed the fewer March gales the ship would encounter and head winds would be less prevalent. Even today the North Atlantic Pilot Chart for the month of March shows that low-powered vessels, and the *City of Glasgow* would have fallen into that category, bound for New York or Philadelphia from the British Isles take the southerly great circle route. Transoceanic vessels rarely sail a straight line from port to port as the layman would think from looking at a map or chart. Winds and currents influence the route that vessels take. Thus, the *City of Glasgow* would have sailed south through the Irish Sea, thence southwest past the Azores down to at least latitude thirty-five degrees north, and then head west. She would have sailed a westerly course at least as far as longitude sixty-five degrees west, which would place her in the vicinity of Bermuda. If she made it this far and was still proceeding toward her destination, she would have changed her heading to a northwesterly course and proceeded on to Delaware Bay—that is, if she had made it through the "Devil's Triangle." For the *City of Glasgow* with her 399 passengers and 81 crewmen had vanished never to be seen or heard from again.

Since Fidel Castro came to power in Cuba, no less than ten thousand refugees have fled that island by sea—that is, ten thousand who have been picked up by coast guard or other vessels. A week doesn't go by that at least one boat or some type of craft isn't spotted drifting northward through the Straits of Florida. These nautical conveyances vary from sailboats to rafts composed of old inner tubes lashed together. Some of these craft are found storm battered and empty. Others are found bullet riddled and empty. It has been estimated that no less than a thousand Cubans have set off from their homeland in some type of small vessel in quest of freedom and were never seen again. Refugees, boats, and all have vanished. To reach the United States mainland from Cuba, one must not only risk being discovered by Cuban patrol boats but also survive the forever-churning waters of the Gulf Stream sweeping through the Straits of Florida and out into the open Atlantic. One couldn't even begin to guess how many refugees have seen Florida's coast disappear behind them as their unmanageable boats or rafts were swept north through the straits and out into the open sea. They would drift on hopelessly, not even the subject of a search. Finally, thirst and hunger would become unbearable. This combined with the torture of the searing sun blistering their salt-crusted bodies beyond human endurance, would drive them mad. And where is there for a madman to go in a small open boat or raft adrift far out in the ocean? Only into the sea whence far back in the chain of life he originally came. This is the "Devil's Triangle."

One wonders how many lives have been needlessly lost in the "Devil's Triangle." Not so much a result of the victims' own doings but because of someone else not wanting to get involved or not caring about another individual in need at sea. Take the example of Talmadge Riggens, A. C. Price, and two other men from Miami. On February 25, 1972, they were fishing from their eighteen-foot boat off the Florida Keys when the engine failed. A west wind blew them out into the Gulf Stream shipping lanes. They were eventually rescued by the coast guard. But even though they were among the lucky ones who might have become four more victims of the "Devil's Triangle," Riggens was still fuming mad when rescued. "We were nearly run down by a tanker whose bridge lookout had us in his searchlight beam. We waved and yelled for help," Riggens said, "but the tanker ignored us and just went on."

There have been similar incidents such as the ordeal of William C. Hoadley, thirty-six, of De Land, Florida, and twenty-year-old Debbie Blocker of Cary, North Carolina. On May 29, 1973, their fifty-foot boat *Tahoma* became disabled eighty miles south of Cuba. With them were two dogs. They had departed from Guana-ha, Spanish Honduras, on May 27. Two days later a fuel line became clogged. The batteries were too weak to start the engine. So for the next forty-two days Hoadley, Debbie, who was pregnant, and the two dogs were adrift in the Caribbean. Using bed sheets, poles, oars, and anything else that he could utilize, Hoadley jury rigged the *Tahoma* with a set of sails. "We drifted from the Cuba area nearly to the U. S. coast, then the Mississippi River pushed us away, and we drifted down to Yucatán. Then we drifted up toward the coastline again, down again to the Campeche Bank, and up almost to New Orleans," Hoadley said.

They collected rainwater and lived off fish during their fifteen-hundred-mile journey. At one time they were within a mile of a Russian trawler about one hundred miles off the Alabama coast. Hoadley kept firing flares, but the Russians ignored him. Finally, some sixty miles southeast of the Mississippi they were sighted by the tugboat *Mary St. Phillip* off Florida and rescued. Hoadley stated that his fiancée's pregnancy was his greatest concern.

William Hoadley's advice to mariners adrift is, "Keep your head. You can panic and kill yourself. Keep your head and work things out. And pray to your favorite god." Although he didn't mention what to pray for, one can be sure that in part it would be that the vessel that sights you isn't like the Russian trawler that ignored the *Tahoma*'s distress flares or the tanker that paid no heed to Talmadge Riggens's plea for help.

There is no doubt that large ships have accounted for a number of so-called disappearances among small craft that never returned to port—particularly disabled boats wallowing helplessly in a running sea.

The fifty-three-foot cabin cruiser *Ixtapa* was due to arrive at Marathon in the Florida Keys for Christmas in 1971. She was returning from a voyage to Cozumel, Mexico. The boat with her owner John Denton and a crew consisting of Richard Spalding, Richard Antonio, and Tom Rash, all of Wilmington, Delaware, never arrived. Attempts to contact the *Ixtapa* by radio were in vain. A search began. For two days nothing was found. On December 28, as darkness approached, the search was suspended for the night. Just as dusk was turning to darkness, and only a glimmer of daylight remained, a vessel spotted a white object almost awash being carried northward by the Gulf Stream's current. The object was taken in tow after being recognized as part of a power boat's cabin. It showed no signs of fire or explosion.

The following day Denton's brother was contacted, but he was unable to identify the wreckage as being positively from the *Ixtapa*. However, further investigation and consultation with the vessel's builder positively identified the debris as being from the missing boat.

There was a considerable amount of speculation among the boatmen along Miami's waterfront as to what happened to the *Ixtapa* and her crew. Conjectures ranged from magnetic phenomenon to having been run down by a ship. A group of occultists raised the question, Why was only the cabin found?

One UFO buff went so far as to say, "Spacemen had to remove the cabin in order to get at the hiding crew." A number of individuals agreed with him. But by far the greatest number of boating men—fishermen, yachtsmen, tugboat men, and the like—adhered to the opinion that the yacht had been run down by a ship that kept going because her crew was completely oblivious to the accident.

Suppose the boat that found the *Ixtapa*'s cabin top had reached that location just a minute or two later when total night had descended upon the area? Or if her course had been just a few yards farther away in either direction leaving the wreckage engulfed in darkness? Then by the following day the Gulf Stream's push would have carried the wreckage many miles to the north where it might never have been found. Then what? Obviously more fuel would have been added to the legend of the "sea of lost ships."

On April 24, 1973, the coast guard announced that it had suspended its search for five men missing off Florida's west coast just north of Florida Bay. Although that area is not considered part of the "Devil's Triangle," conditions there are very similar with the exception of the prevailing wind direction and the fact that the Gulf Stream does not flow there. Certain situations can make this area as hazardous. The prevailing winds are actually from the same direction, southeast, but rather than being onshore as on the state's east coast, they are offshore. Thus, a vessel that has become disabled in water too deep for anchoring could be blown far out into the Gulf of Mexico.

Four of the five missing men, William Forshee; his son William, Jr.; De Witt Lewis; and a Mr. Gaskin were from the Miami area. They had set off from Marco Island in their eighteen-foot outboard for a day's fishing.

The fifth man, Robert Stone of Fort Myers, had gone fishing in his fourteen-foot outboard on April 7. Eleven aircraft and numerous boats operated by the coast guard and coast guard auxiliary searched more than 16,000 square miles in an operation that extended 150 miles out into the Gulf of Mexico. But searchers were unable to locate the two boats or the five men in them.

As mentioned previously, the United States Coast Guard rescues refugees fleeing from Cuba almost on a regular schedule. But there is another dictatorship that is also driving its victims to desperation in an attempt to flee its regime.

In the Old Bahama Channel that separates the Bahamas from Cuba on July 17, 1973, eighteen Haitian refugees were rescued from their sinking boat on a voyage to freedom. Their floundering boat sank as it was being towed to Miami by the fishing boat that rescued the escapees.

A crewman and spokesman for the group, thirty-three-year-old Georges Pierre, told of the ordeal suffered by the refugees, who included twelve women. He told of the hot beating sun, the loss of their drinking water, continuous bailing to keep afloat, and the constant praying. "They called God many times, and some claimed they spoke to Him," he said. "They said He said, 'Be patient, I'll get you where you want to go.' I was not so sure." Pierre went on, "All aboard had to bail more and more as the calking between the hull planks fell out.

"But the other boat . . . it disappeared during the second night," Pierre said. Then he told of a second boat that accompanied the one he was on. Forty-five of his companions were jam-packed aboard a twenty-two-foot sloop. They were in sight of each other and talked back and forth for two days. They were never more than a few hundred yards apart. On the second night when only three boat lengths separated the two vessels, a pall of silence fell over the two boats.

Nearly everyone aboard Pierre's boat was asleep. Those manning the boat and bailing thought everyone on the other boat was sleeping; hence, they paid little notice to it. Then they discovered that the other boat was gone. At first they thought it might have drifted off into the darkness and they would see it in a few hours when dawn came. But as day broke, the sea was empty from horizon to horizon. They didn't even see a piece of wreckage. At first Pierre thought the other boat must have foundered for it was loaded to within four inches of the gunwale. "But then," Pierre said, "we did not hear any screams for help or that they were in trouble. There was just silence."

Yes, just silence. Forty-five souls so desperate for freedom that without qualms they boarded the little twenty-two-foot sloop. They were so crowded that most could only stand. They knew that their chances of finding freedom were slim, but anything was better than the lives they had been living. So they put out to sea. Instead of finding life, liberty, and the pursuit of happiness, they found only the "Devil's Triangle."

George Boston's claim to fame was that he played football at Harvard with Bobby Kennedy and was the first Harvard freshman ever to score a touchdown against Yale. But George Boston's first love was the sea. He was invited to try out for the Dodger's baseball team at its spring training session. The pitcher wound up and pitched. There was a "crrraack." Astounded veterans and awed rookies jumped up. George Boston had hit a home run his first time at bat. But, again, George Boston's first love was the sea, and it was the sea that he chose. It was a simple matter of love before money. He wrote for various yachting and sailing magazines, had a weekly yachting column in the Boston *Globe*, and lectured to various clubs and yachting groups on the fine art of blue water sailing. His friends described him as "a big, hefty, likable guy who sailed by the seat of his pants." He became renowned in sailing circles for his single-handed cruises.

His most ambitious endeavor, a solo circumnavigation in a thirty-foot Tahiti ketch, ended when he came down with hepatitis in Egypt. Even though that attempt ended in failure, fame and admiration followed George Boston wherever he sailed his little white ketch *Fiddler's Green*, which, ironically, is the mythical heaven where all good sailors go when they embark on their final voyage.

George Boston's last voyage was not aboard the *Fiddler's Green*. After his return from the Mediterranean, he set out again, alone, sailing through the West Indies. It was on this voyage that he met and married a girl sailor. They sailed back to Florida where they bought a modest yellow-and-white house alongside a canal lined with sailboats in Fort Lauderdale. His main source of income was from skippering and delivering yachts. His spare time was spent writing a book about his experiences aboard *Fiddler's Green*. Although there was a last chapter, George Boston would not write it.

In October, 1965, Fort Lauderdale yacht broker Jan D. Bragg engaged Boston's services to deliver a forty-five-foot catamaran-type houseboat to Enrique Blanco in San Juan, Puerto Rico. The *El Gato* had, according to Bragg, "plenty of gear on board including a dinghy with an outboard motor." The trip was to be a routine island-hopping delivery along a route that Boston had sailed many times before.

On October 16, Boston told his wife Margaret that he would be back in ten days if the weather stayed good and the boat's engine operated properly. He kissed her good-bye, boarded the *El Gato*, which is Spanish for "The Cat," made a last-minute inspection, and cast off for sea.

The first leg of the journey was from Fort Lauderdale to Nassau. However, the first day out the boat developed engine trouble and Boston brought her into Nassau limping along at four knots. The *El Gato* lay in Nassau for several days while the engine was being repaired. Bragg sent Boston some money to pay the repair bill, and once again, on October 23, *El Gato* was under way to her next stopover, Georgetown in the Exumas. It was reported overdue on October 27. But the boat was quickly located the next day at Great Exuma anchored in one of that island's many harbors within a harbor. Boston had stopped off to visit with friends.

On October 28, Boston departed, supposedly, but never substantiated, with a native crewman. The *El Gato*'s next stop was to be Great Inagua Island.

The *El Gato* never reached there. Six coast guard aircraft searched the area. Seas were fairly calm during the search, but the coast guard reported sixteen-to twenty-foot seas at the time the *El Gato* disappeared. The search was concentrated in the 135-mile area between Great Inagua and Grand Turk islands. After several days of fruitless probing in these waters, the hunt was extended to all of the southern Bahamas, Cuba, Haiti, Dominican Republic, Puerto Rico, and down through the Windward Passage. After two weeks the operation was called off. However, all military aircraft were requested to maintain a surveillance for the missing boat.

Back in Fort Lauderdale, the sailing fraternity, most of whom knew the forty-three-year-old transatlantic sailor, laid odds that he would show up again sooner or later. Mrs. Boston, who had sailed a number of times with her husband in the area where he was lost, commented, "I am sure he's all right. The engine wasn't in good shape when he left, but he's a resourceful man. So he is probably sitting under a palm tree on an island fixing the carburetor or something."

Yes, on an island thousands of miles away from the gridirons of the Ivy League, the first Harvard freshman football player ever to score a touchdown against Yale "is probably sitting under a palm tree fixing a carburetor or something"—that is, if there are palm trees and carburetors in Fiddler's Green.

5. The *Cyclops*

Just like her namesake, the mythical lumbering one-eyed giant, the U.S.S. *Cyclops* was ruled by one eye and one eye only—Lieutenant Commander George W. Worley. This twentieth-century Captain Bligh characteristically paced back and forth the length of the flying bridge, carrying a cane, wearing a derby hat, dressed in long underwear, and savagely chewing the end of a cigar. Had Jack London ever met him, it would have been George Worley and not Wolf Larsen in command of the schooner *Ghost* in his literary classic *The Sea-Wolf*. Silhouetted against the full moon one could have mistaken Worley for a gorilla pacing the ship's bridge. And here looks were not deceiving, for he possessed the strength of three men as his crew had found out on more than one occasion. Each stride was deliberate, and with every step his foot became part of the deck. Every movement of muscle from the sway of his shoulders to the contorting of his lips purling around the cigar was in unison with the heave of the *Cyclops* as she steamed away from Norfolk with a cargo of coal, mail, and supplies destined for a fleet of United States warships stationed off the east coast of South America in January, 1918.

The huge 19,000-ton coaling ship, her hull pressed low in the water by the bulk of her cargo, rolled sluggishly as she departed the frigid waters of the North Atlantic and plied southward through the warm tropical waters of the northward-flowing Gulf Stream. Her crew, those not on watch or sacked out in their bunks below, lined the rail at the ship's bow mystified by the effect of the prow slicing through the phosphorescent glazed sea. At times one or another of the men would cast an uneasy glance at the shadow pacing the flying bridge. Those who had sailed with Captain Worley before knew that this was a "hell ship." However, there was no awareness among them or their master that the *Cyclops* was entering the most mysterious area of all the seven seas—the "Devil's Triangle."

The crew, both officers and men, whether right or wrong, dared not stand up to this walking hurricane. But like the barracuda forever ferreting a coral reef for its prey, Worley too had to have a victim. This voyage it was a young officer, Ensign Cain, who as a result of the captain's harassing, was placed in the ship's sick bay by Dr. Burt J. Aspen, the ship's surgeon, to prevent his becoming completely demented. Yet, there was one man aboard the collier who would face down the commanding officer. He was Lieutenant Harvey Forbes, the executive officer. But he too was destined to fall before the wrath of the master.

"Sometimes I thought Captain Worley was born fifty years or even a century too late. He was a perfect example of the tyrannical bucko sailing-ship captains who considered their crews not as human beings but only as a means of getting their vessels to the next port. He was a gruff eccentric salt of the old

school given to carrying a cane but possessing few
other qualities. He was a very indifferent seaman and
a poor, overly cautious navigator . . . unfriendly and
taciturn, generally disliked by both his officers and
his men." These are the words of Conrad Nervig, who
as an ensign in 1918, was the last crew member to
leave the *Cyclops* before she sailed to oblivion.

"I first met Captain Worley in November of 1917
when I reported aboard the *Cyclops*. He seemed a nice
gentleman. It was only later that I discovered his pe-
culiarities. He would visit me on the bridge during
my dog watch [midnight to 4 A.M.] carrying a cane,
dressed in long underwear, and wearing a derby hat.
He would lean on the bridge rail looking at the sea
ahead and talking of his family and children, but he
was quite erratic at times. Without the slightest pause
between words, his mood would change to that of a
very opinionated man—a self-proclaimed genius who
thought he had never arrived but should have. It was
while in these moods that he'd take out his rage on
some unknowing officer. Although he treated me very
well—he seemed to like me—why?—I don't know. It
was part of his makeup. When it came time for me
to leave the ship, he tried to get the admiral of the
South Atlantic Patrol Fleet to have me stay. Fortu-
nately I got away, or I wouldn't be here now."

And how right Nervig was, for had Worley been
able to keep him on the ship, there would have been
no one at hand fifty-two years later when Nervig
stood before a camera telling about life aboard the
Cyclops for the documentary film *The Devil's Triangle*.

"One of the bad features on that ship was the gloom
in the wardroom. It was such a depressing place due
to the strange behavior of the captain. Everyone was
unhappy. It was a relief to take my watch on the

bridge with nothing but the moonlight and the nice balmy weather. It was a great sedative after the depression down below."

Captain Worley brought the ship that he had commanded since it was built in 1910 through the "Devil's Triangle." But it was a voyage not without incident. "So many unusual things happened to the *Cyclops* on her trip to South America," Nervig went on. "First in leaving Norfolk Navy Yard she almost had a collision with the U.S.S. *Survey* outward bound for antisubmarine duty in the Mediterranean, the head blew off one of the engines—this meant we had to finish the trip on one engine—she sailed past the port of Rio, and only daylight saved her from going up on the rocks. Then there was the poor seaman who was drowned after being hit by one of the ship's propellers. Then after coaling the cruiser *Raleigh*, she scraped the side of that ship causing some damage." Completely oblivious to the lights and camera, Nervig continued almost as though he had been physically conveyed back in time over half a century. "All of this I attribute to Worley's poor navigation and his poor seamanship. Our close call with the rocks off Rio was a perfect example. Lieutenant Forbes had already plotted our course for that port. The captain made some changes, which resulted in our near catastrophe. When Forbes confronted Worley about why he changed his course and nearly wrecked the ship, Worley exploded and had Forbes immediately placed under arrest and confined to quarters." But this time the *Cyclops* reached her destination—Rio de Janeiro.

A month earlier when Nervig first reported aboard the *Cyclops* on November 21, 1917, there occurred an incident aboard the U.S.S. *Pittsburgh*, anchored in the harbor at Rio, that could possibly have influenced the future fate of the *Cyclops*.

The *Pittsburgh* was the flagship of the South American Patrol Fleet and under the command of Captain George B. Bradshaw. Before reporting to station off the east coast of South America, the *Pittsburgh* served with the navy's Pacific Fleet based at San Francisco. She was there when the United States entered World War I. A number of San Francisco street "toughs" joined the navy, for one reason or the other, and were assigned to Captain Bradshaw's ship. They were quite clannish and formed the nucleus of an undesirable element aboard the cruiser, a situation common when large groups of men are brought together under conditions of stress. Most were assigned below deck in the engine and firerooms where they bullied most of their shipmates including some of the petty officers.

On the same date that Ensign Nervig joined the *Cyclops* in Norfolk, a number of the "San Francisco gang" were gathered in one of the *Pittsburgh*'s boiler rooms. Most of the ship's crew were ashore on liberty, but the San Franciscans either elected to remain aboard or were restricted to the ship for disciplinary reasons. Also in the fireroom were a petty officer and an on-duty fireman maintaining the fire in boiler number six. Shortly after 11 P.M., the group was joined by Fireman First Class James Coker and Fireman Second Class Barney De Voe. The pair had brought with them a quantity of liquor. It wasn't long before tempers and inhibitions were near an end.

Homosexuality was a minor problem in the "old" navy. Although not prevalent, it did exist. Among the group was a young Texan, Fireman Third Class Oscar Stewart, who although not actually accepted by the "gang," was tolerated by them, probably because Stewart would at times respond favorably to homosexual advances in exchange for candy and other favors. To this day some of the old-timers in the navy refer to candy bars as "pogey bait" in a joking manner. Apparently several weeks previously Coker and De Voe had made advances to Stewart, who rejected them with the excuse that he had contracted gonorrhea from a girl that he had met. He explained that he didn't report to the ship's sick bay for fear of being disciplined, and he didn't have enough money to seek medical attention ashore. Coker and De Voe dug into their pockets and came up with sufficient money for him to get treatment from a private doctor in Rio de Janeiro. Stewart did not see the two men again until the night of the party in fireroom number six.

Petty Officer Moss Whiteside was in charge of the watch and actually took part in the drinking. At midnight Whiteside was relieved by Petty Officer John Morefield, who although he did not participate in the party, did nothing to stop it, probably out of fear. As the night advanced, most of the celebrants staggered off to their quarters. Among those who remained were De Voe, Coker, and Stewart. Drunkenly working their way over to where Stewart sat, Coker and De Voe propositioned the tipsy Texan. As the story goes, after the homosexual act was over, Stewart began laughing about the fact that he had spent the money on more whores and now the three of them had something in common. Before the echo of his laughter had vanished, the two Californians were upon him with fists flying. Morefield, the only sober individual left, broke up the fight and went about his duties. All was quiet except for the roar of the boiler's fire and the hiss of steam. When Morefield went up to the second level to check a leaking pump, Coker and De Voe dragged the unconscious Stewart behind one of the boilers. Fearing that their victim might spread the word about the homosexual act and the venereal disease, Coker started beating the Texan about the head with a hammer while De Voe stood lookout. By the time Morefield returned to the lower level, the two culprits had hidden their victim and sneaked out of the fireroom via an emergency exit. Their plan was to return later, cut the Texan into pieces small enough to fit into the firebox under the boiler, and let the flames dispose of the body.

During the next watch, a messenger passing through the fireroom heard a moaning noise from somewhere under the catwalk he was crossing. Upon investigation he discovered Stewart behind the boiler with his head pulverized to a bloody pulp. Realizing that the hapless crewman was still alive, the messenger went for help. Stewart was taken to the *Pittsburgh*'s sick bay where he remained unconscious. Learning that their victim had been found alive, the two assailants decided they'd better get going while the getting was good. After pocketing a collection of money coerced from various individuals of the crew by other members of the gang, Coker and De Voe departed from the flagship in style: they stole the captain's gig. Their freedom was short-lived, however. Rumors of two non-Portugese-speaking strangers brought the authorities storming into their mountainside hideout.

Stewart lingered on for nearly a month without ever gaining consciousness. With his death, murder charges were brought against Coker and De Voe, and they were placed under double security in the ship's brig. Also placed under arrest were Petty Officers Whiteside and Morefield. Whiteside was charged with both participating in and not stopping a drunken party. Morefield was confined for not reporting a drunken party.

The courts-martial commenced the day before Christmas. Coker was found guilty of murder and sentenced to death by hanging. De Voe was sentenced to fifty to ninety-nine years in prison for his complicity in the murder. Whiteside received a fifteen-year sentence for not reporting or stopping a drunken party, participating in a drunken party, and perjury. Morefield, who was not a member of the gang, had an unblemished service record, and had already been recommended for a promotion, was given five years for not stopping a drunken party. All but Coker were to be transported to the Naval Prison at Portsmouth, New Hampshire, "by the first available transportation."

A month later, on January 28, the *Cyclops* arrived at Rio. Included in his orders when Worley reported to the flagship the following day were instructions for him to receive five court-martialed prisoners. In addition to those involved in Stewart's murder, there were two marine privates, named Stamey and Hill, each sentenced to two years for being AWOL. Worley's reaction to this situation is unknown. The only thing that the prisoners knew about the *Cyclops* before they boarded her was that "the brig at Portsmouth wouldn't be as bad as Worley's ship." The *Cyclops* cruised Brazilian waters through most of February.

On Sunday, February 3, the *Pittsburgh* was preparing to put to sea. Forty-two men from the cruiser, who were being sent back to the United States for reassignment, were transferred to the *Cyclops* as passengers. A number of these transferees had been friends of Coker and De Voe. Upon their arrival aboard the collier, they found the prisoners on deck handcuffed and wearing leg irons. Armed guards were posted around the vessel. Worley was wearing a forty-five. Rumors flew about the ship: the passengers from the *Pittsburgh* would try to free their former shipmates; Lieutenant Forbes was still under arrest, and the crew, once at sea, would seize the ship and free their executive officer; the prisoners had it better than the crew; Worley was going mad; Coker was to be transferred to the *Cyclops* for his execution. Every incident, no matter how minor, became fuel for the rumor mill that the *Cyclops* had become.

After watching the *Pittsburgh* head out to sea, the *Cyclops*'s passengers discovered that Commander Worley was not wearing the forty-five automatic because of the contingent of prisoners or his incarcerated executive officer. This was punishment day —a day in which those accused of infractions of the ship's (and Worley's) rules were to pay for their misdeeds. As their shipmates watched from an "at ease" position, the accused were lined up at attention and Worley read the list of violations. All would be restricted to the ship. But those who had been before the captain previously were ordered to remove their shoes and stockings. Then at pistol point Worley drove the barefoot men around the ship's sun-scorched steel decks. After a circuit around the ship, the men would return to their original starting place where a seaman with a fire hose washed down their feet with cool seawater. That same day the *Cyclops* weighed anchor and moved alongside a bulk cargo dock where she was to take on approximately eleven thousand tons of manganese ore.

Manganese is a grayish white metallic substance that when added to other metals gives them a substantial increase in strength. Naval guns, large and small, are fabricated from manganese bronze. Ships' propellers and propeller shafts are also made of manganese bronze. The ore has a tremendous weight per cubic foot when compared to coal, which the *Cyclops* normally carried; thus, the ship's holds were to be loaded by weight rather than volume. Manganese is an abrasive material that has a tendency to settle down creating a grinding action on whatever might be under it. For these reasons, extra-heavy shorings and bracings must be used to prevent the cargo from shifting or reacting to the roll of the ship. Only one officer aboard the *Cyclops* was experienced in handling this type of cargo—Lieutenant Forbes, who before entering the naval service had spent a number of years on the Great Lakes as master of vessels specializing in the transportation of heavy ores. But Forbes was still under arrest and confined to his quarters. To supervise the loading Worley assigned a new young ensign with little experience in loading coal let alone an exotic cargo such as manganese ore.

Inch by inch the *Cyclops*'s hull settled deeper in the water as ton after ton of the heavy bulk cargo poured into her seven gaping holds. While the ship was being loaded, Nervig received orders transferring him to the U.S.S. *Glacier*, a supply ship. Receiving word of the transfer, Worley, who had been drinking heavily, became quite angry. Nervig's transfer meant he was losing one of his few experienced officers and probably the only man aboard with whom he was able to communicate. Worley contacted the admiral of the South Atlantic Patrol Fleet in an attempt to keep Nervig aboard the *Cyclops*. But to Nervig's relief, the orders were not rescinded.

The captain was probably better known by Nervig than by anyone else aboard the ship. As Nervig recalled a half century later, "He visited me every night when I had the dog watch [midnight to 4 A.M.]. These

Forever Lost?

Mysterious Victims of the
"Devil's Triangle"

The sleek racing yawl *Revonoc* disappeared almost within sight of Miami with the publisher Harvey Conover, Sr. and his wife on board.

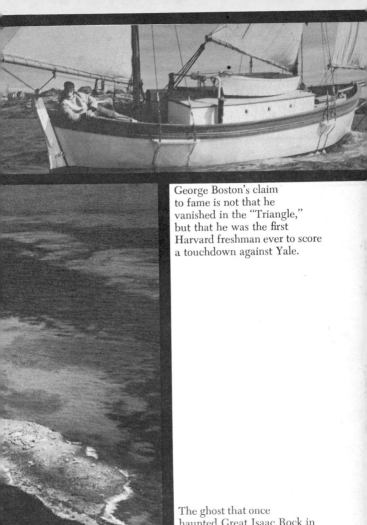

George Boston's claim to fame is not that he vanished in the "Triangle," but that he was the first Harvard freshman ever to score a touchdown against Yale.

The ghost that once haunted Great Isaac Rock in the Bahamas has long since gone. But the rock is still in the "Devil's Triangle," and during Christmas week in 1967, two lighthouse keepers simply vanished without a trace.
(BAHAMAS NEWS BUREAU, PHOTO BY FREDERIC MAURA)

The Japanese crew of the *Raifuku Maru* discovered the strange happenings in the Caribbean were more than legend. The last that was ever heard from the freighter was the code message: "Danger like dagger now. Come quick!" Is the waterspout—a tornado at sea—the mystery behind the "Devil's Triangle?"

(WIDE WORLD)

The S.S. *Marine Sulphur Queen* is one of the "Triangle's" more noted victims. But was its disappearance really an unexplainable mystery? Coast Guardsmen examine the trail board from the *Marine Sulphur Queen*.

On December 5, 1945, five
Navy Avengers took
off from Fort Lauderdale
Naval Air Station and were
never seen again.
Aboard were fourteen men.
(U. S. NAVY)

The *Cyclops'* captain was Lt. Comm. George W. Worley, shown here aboard the ship while the vessel was in Norfolk.
(U.S. NAVY)

The largest single loss of life in recent years in the "Triangle" occurred when the *U.S.S. Cyclops* vanished with 309 officers and men. This is the last known picture taken of the *Cyclops,* snapped on January 7, 1918, the day before the collier left Norfolk for the last time.

Could a brutal murder that occurred deep down in the bowels of the *U.S.S. Pittsburgh* have ultimately led to the strange disappearance of the *Cyclops?*
(U. S. NAVY)

The *Nereus* and *Proteus*, two sister ships of the *Cyclops*, vanished in the "Devil's Triangle" late in 1941. Their disappearance was overshadowed by the United States' entry into World War II.

The author filming aboard the research submarine
Ben Franklin as it begins its
descent into the depths of the "Triangle."

Miami Coast Guard Rescue
Center Controller,
Lt. Miles, monitoring the
search operation
for Dr. Fischer.
(U. S. COAST GUARD)

A rescue helicopter
leaves the deck of the
cutter *Dauntless*
before first light
during the search
for a missing single
engine plane carrying
Dr. Robert Fischer, his
wife and two daughters.
(U. S. COAST GUARD)

The helicopter
radioed back that they
had found a possible
clue to the
Fischers' fate.
(U. S. COAST GUARD)

The *Dauntless* with bridge lookouts scanning for a trace
of the Fischer family or their plane in the "Devil's Triangle."
(U. S. COAST GUARD

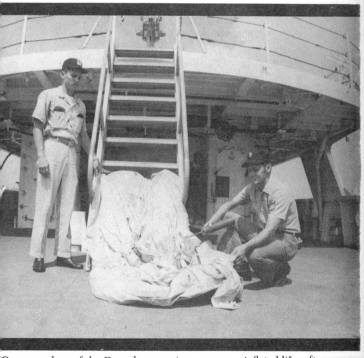
Crew members of the *Dauntless* examine an open uninflated life raft that might or might not have come from the Fischers' aircraft.

"Finally thirst and hunger would become unbearable. This, combined with the torture of the sun blistering their salt crusted bodies, would drive them stark raving mad. And where is there for a mad man to go in a small open raft far out in an empty ocean? Only into the sea . . . for this is the 'Devil's Triangle'."

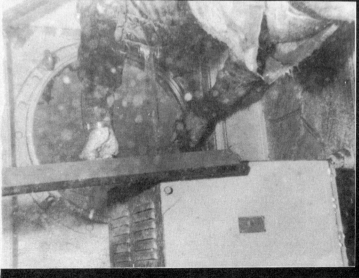

Contrary to the fable that when divers found the doomed tanker V. A. *Fogg*, all bodies were missing except that of the captain's, here is an official Coast Guard photograph of the helmsman's body floating inside the ship's wheelhouse
(U. S. COAST GUARD)

visits lasted some two hours, and as we leaned against the forward bridge rail, he regaled me with stories of his home and numerous incidents of his long life at sea. He had a fund of tales, mostly humorous. These nocturnal visits became a regular routine, and I rather enjoyed them. His uniform, if it could be so called, never varied from the long underwear he had worn on that first occasion. I have often wondered to what I owed these visits—his fondness for me or his sleeplessness." Nervig was to see the *Cyclops* once more.

The next several days were spent by the collier's crew preparing the big ship for sea. As the water level neared her Plimsoll mark, hatches were battened down. But loading continued and eventually the hull was immersed to a point where the Plimsoll mark was under water, signifying that the ship was overloaded. Why this was permitted remains a mystery. It had to be more than an oversight, for even the least experienced seaman knows this is dangerous. Upon completion of loading and preparation for sea, the *Cyclops* cast off and headed up the coast to Bahia.

As in other areas south of the equator, February is midsummer in Brazil. It is the rainy season. On February 21, Lieutenant Nervig was standing at the bow of the *Glacier*, which was anchored in the harbor at Bahia. Dressed in yellow foul-weather gear, he was unrecognizable from the four enlisted men next to him. It had been drizzling steadily for several days. They had gone forward for a routine check of the ship's anchor chain. Looking seaward, Nervig saw the grayish black skeletal superstructure of the *Cyclops* looming through the haze. Her twenty-four coaling booms were secured in seagoing position, the clamshell coal scoops were chained in place on deck, and all of her boats lashed to their skids. The *Cyclops*

was ready for her long voyage home. What did Nervig think as he watched his former ship pushing
against the outgoing tide? "As Bahia lies north of Rio
de Janeiro, the *Cyclops* should have been seen coming from the south. But she stood in from the north.
Again the familiar example of navigation as practiced
aboard that vessel." The collier drifted to a halt, and
the tranquil sound of the gentle pelting rain was shattered by the clatter of chain hurtling through the
ship's hawsepipe. The *Cyclops* was at anchor.

Everyone who has ever served in the military can
recall one friend or buddy whose memory stands out
in his mind above that of anyone else regardless of
how many years have gone by. Over a half century
has transpired since Conrad Nervig last saw his "best
friend," Ensign Carrol G. Page, the *Cyclops*'s paymas-
ter. Page was the nephew of Senator Page, chairman
of the Senate Naval Committee, and a scion of one
of America's most politically prominent families. He
had entered the navy as a commissioned officer, while
Nervig was a mustang (naval terminology for one
who has worked his way up from the ranks to a commission), who had joined the navy in 1907. In spite
of their disparate backgrounds, they spent hours discussing everything from Nervig's experiences in the
"old navy" of the prewar days to Page's Ivy League college adventures.

The *Cyclops* had orders to sail for Baltimore on
the following day, February 22. That day Ensign Page
went aboard the *Glacier* to sign for some supplies issued to the *Cyclops*. This was the last time that Nervig
saw his friend. "At his departure, I, as officer of the
deck, escorted him to the gangway. On leaving, he
grasped my hand in both of his, and said very solemn-
ly, 'Well, good-bye, old man, and God bless you.' I

was deeply impressed with his finality, which was truly prophetic in its implication. I never saw Ensign Page again."

Yet one more element was to be added to the already bizarre ship's complement before the *Cyclops*'s departure. Following a celebration at a private villa in Bahia, Consul General Alfred L. M. Gottschalk was driven to the navy pier in a 1916 Pierce-Arrow touring car. Waiting for the car was a motor whaleboat from the *Cyclops*. Standing in the stern sheets was Ensign Page who had just been picked up at the *Glacier*. Also aboard was the regular four-man crew, who immediately upon arrival of the car started loading Gottschalk's trunks, bags, and suitcases aboard. After taking leave of friends who accompanied him to the dock, the consul general boarded the boat and was on his way out to the *Cyclops*.

Gottschalk boarded the gangway and climbed to the ship's main deck where he was greeted by Worley wearing dress whites and completely unconcerned about the light rain that was erasing the press and creases of his uniform as he stepped out from under the shelter of the deckhouse. Most of the crew were quite mindful of the weather, for they had been lined up in it wearing their dress uniforms for some time awaiting the consul general. The dignitary was shown his quarters and the crew allowed to break ranks. As the whaleboat was hoisted aboard, a bos'n mate opened the main steam valve to the anchor winch. In a matter of minutes the ker-lunking noise of the machine was drowned out by the clanking of the anchor chain coming back up through the hawsepipe. The ship was already vibrating to the throb of the propellers chopping through the water. In a matter of minutes the ship had come about and was heading seaward—taking 309 men on a voyage that would become the strangest unsolved mystery of the sea.

Lieutenant Nervig stood on the *Glacier's* bridge watching the *Cyclops* standing out to sea. As he watched the ship disappear into the rain, he thought of the portent finality of his friend's farewell. With the last glimpse of the vessel before she was swallowed up in the rain, Nervig muttered aloud, "I bet there isn't a crewman aboard her who wouldn't give anything to change places with me right now."

By dawn the next day the *Cyclops*, steaming north, was no longer within sight of land. Her orders were to proceed directly to Baltimore. She had taken aboard more than adequate coal and provisions for the journey. An early riser, Gottschalk was on deck at daybreak admiring the sun's ascension above the cloud-lined horizon, a spectacle that prevails only in tropical and subtropical oceans. As the sun's intemperate heat began to overwhelm the lingering night-cooled air, the consul general sauntered down to the wardroom where he joined the ship's officers at breakfast. It was here that he became aware of the number of unusual circumstances concerning his forty-seven fellow passengers, the *Cyclops*, and her crew. He had known of the murder aboard the *Pittsburgh*, but it was only now that he learned that three of those involved were aboard the ship. He was introduced to Lieutenant Forbes who although still under arrest was permitted to eat with the officers. As the day wore on, he gradually became aware of an air of general discontent amid the crew. A homeward-bound crew should be a happy crew, not these tense, dispirited men. And although it was traditional for a naval vessel to fly a homeward-bound pennant from her masthead during her passage home, the *Cyclops* flew none.

As the *Cyclops* made her way north, she was still a principal topic of conversation at the officers' club and waterfront bars in Brazil. She was the subject of numerous rumors. One in particular was that the deserters would try to mutiny. Could this be more than hearsay? Or was it typical navy scuttlebutt in which the five prisoners were amplified into a large number of mutineers? If it was but rumor, what motivated it?

The *Cyclops* continued northward but at a reduced speed, for the starboard engine, probably as a result of inadequate repairs in Rio de Janeiro, had again broken down. With only the port engine, her sustained speed was eight knots. Captain Worley had been drinking almost to excess. He had been known throughout the fleet as a man who could match any man glass for glass and get up and walk out seemingly unaffected. What caused him to guzzle as his crew had not seen him do before? Could it have been the trouble-plagued starboard engine? Could it be the thought of the vessel's being overloaded? Then too there were the prisoners from the *Pittsburgh* and their friends among the passengers. The *Pittsburgh*'s commanding officer, Captain Bradshaw, had warned him not to take any chances. Did something occur among the prisoners involving some of the passengers and possibly some malcontent members of Worley's crew? Although the ship had departed Brazil with more than enough coal and supplies to reach her destination, and Worley had orders to proceed directly to Baltimore without any stops, the vessel failed to do so.

Barbados is the easternmost island of the West Indies. Beyond her to the east lies nothing but open sea almost all of the way to the Canary Islands just off the coast of Africa. At the western end of the island is its largest city, Bridgetown, which overlooks Carlisle Bay. On Sunday, March 3, the *Cyclops* entered Carlisle Bay. The reverberations of the ship's anchor chain surging through the hawsepipe brought the townspeople scurrying to the waterfront, because it was a rare occasion for a vessel the size of this one to visit the island. The small harbor would not accommodate vessels the size and draft of the *Cyclops,* thus the ship rode anchor about a mile offshore. From her yardarm she flew an English flag as a standard nautical courtesy to this British possession. As soon as her identity was known to the island's officials, Brockholst Livingston, the United States consul at Barbados, boarded a launch along with customs officers and other island functionaries and headed out to the collier. After the usual handshaking and introduction rituals, Livingston accompanied Worley to the captain's cabin under the ship's bridge. It was here that the consul was informed that the reason for the ship's unscheduled call was due to a need for money, coal, and supplies in order to complete the voyage home.

Although the relationship between Worley and the counsul was mostly cordial, some words must have been exchanged when the former insisted on taking aboard large stores of foodstuff despite protests by Livingston about the price and quantity.

After his meeting with Livingston and the completion of the routine customs check, Worley had some of the ship's boats launched and permitted members of the crew to have an eight-hour liberty. Apparently the men who went ashore during the ship's two-day stopover caused little trouble and all returned to the ship. But they did talk, for every bartender and anyone who was anyone on the island knew of the executive officer's duress, the prisoners, the mechanical troubles, the crew's dislike of their captain, and hints of certain other odd happenings aboard the *Cyclops*.

The next afternoon, Livingston invited Worley, Gottschalk, and the ship's surgeon, Burt J. Aspen, to the consulate for tea. The affair was most cordial. There was no hint of any danger during the rest of the voyage and the men from the ship seemed eager to be home. Before leaving, the three men signed the consul's daughter's autograph book. When the consul's young son, Brockholst Livingston III, returned from school, Worley told him all about the ship and life in the navy. A number of years later, young Livingston recalled, "About five o'clock our guests left, and we watched them from the beach as they went on board. There were some blasts on the whistles, and the *Cyclops* backed. Then going ahead, she steamed *south*. We did not consider this course odd until a few weeks later. We got a cable from the State Department requesting full details of her visit to Barbados." This was the last that was ever seen of the big ship, Worley, his crew, Gottschalk, the other passengers and the prisoners of the *Cyclops*. All that is known is that the *Cyclops* had again entered the "Devil's Triangle."

The next day, March 5, the British liner *Vestris*, operated by Lampert and Holt Lines, exchanged radio communications with the *Cyclops*. The latter reported "fair weather" and indicated no difficulties. The *Cyclops* was never heard from again. The United States Navy's largest collier was reported overdue on March 13, and immediately an intensive sea search was un-

der way. Thousands and thousands of miles of the Atlantic Ocean were probed but no trace of the ship was
ever found.

In response to the cable to Livingston, the State
Department received a most shocking reply:

Secretary of State
Washington
April 17, 2 P.M.

Department's 15th. Confidential. Master Cyclops stated
that required 600 tons coal having sufficient to reach
Bermuda. Engines very poor condition. Not sufficient
funds and therefore requested payment by me—unusual.
I have ascertained that he took here ton fresh meat, ton
flour, thousand pounds vegetables, paying therefore 775
dollars. From different sources have learned the following.
He had plenty of coal, alleged inferior; took coal, probably
more than fifteen hundred tons. Master alluded to by
others as damned Dutchman, apparently disliked by other
officers. Rumored disturbances en route hither, men confined and one executed; also conspired [with] some
prisoners from fleet in Brazilian waters, one [with] life
sentence. United States Consul General Gottschalk passenger. 231 crew exclusive of officers and passengers.
Have names [of] crew but not of all officers and passengers. Many Germanic names appear. Number tele-
graphic or wireless messages addressed master or in care
of ship were delivered at this port. All telegrams for
Barbados on file head office St. Thomas. I have to sug-
gest scrutinizing these. While not having any definite
grounds, I fear fate worse than sinking, though possibly
based on instinctive dislike felt towards master.

LIVINGSTON, CONSUL

It is possible that a clue to the *Cyclops*'s disappearance is contained in Livingston's cable to the State
Department. Studying the cable segment by segment,
these strange facts merit comment.

1. Captain Worley requested six hundred tons of

coal, yet when actual coaling took place, fifteen hundred tons were loaded aboard the *Cyclops*.

2. He stated that he needed six hundred tons to reach Bermuda. But why Bermuda? The safest and most practical route would be to skirt the Windward Islands, the Virgin Islands, Puerto Rico, Dominica, and eastern Cuba with the help of the following seas created by the easterly trade winds and then utilize the push of the Gulf Stream's four-knot northward current through the Straits of Florida. Why risk voyaging out into the open Atlantic during wartime? Especially during March when strong northeasterly winds are the rule rather than the exception and particularly with only one engine operational?

3. The poor condition of the ship's engines and machinery could completely disable the vessel at sea. But she had several complete sets of standby power batteries with which to operate the radio in such an emergency.

4. The additional provisions would not necessarily be of any significance even though the ship was fully provisioned upon departure from Brazil. A ton each of meat and flour would not go far among 308 men (assuming one was executed).

5. Had there been an execution aboard the *Cyclops*, it would have been the first navy shipboard hanging since 1849. However, would Worley have carried out an execution without a general court-martial and presidential approval? By law, both would be required. Livingston reported only a rumor. Yet rare is the rumor that doesn't have at least a grain of truth to it.

6. Livingston also reported rumored disturbances at sea. Consider the circumstances: a tyrannical ship's master, a skilled and well-liked officer unjustly under arrest, hardened prisoners having nothing to lose in

an escape attempt, men aboard whose friends and former shipmates were imprisoned on the same ship, seamen seeing a shipmate illegally executed (if such an event did take place), and a general atmosphere of tension prevailing over the *Cyclops*. Almost anything could happen. Did anything happen? Or did Worley deliberately sail the *Cyclops* on a voyage of self-destruction? Unknown to him, he was scheduled to face a Board of Inquiry about his imperious treatment of his crew on his return. But he would have known the consequences to himself if an execution took place.

7. Although not mentioned in the consul's telegram, the ship was last seen heading *south*, which would be away from her destination. Was this the captain's deliberate decision or "again the familiar example of navigation as practiced aboard that vessel"? It might even have been in conjunction with a routine compass check in the manner done on large ships to determine if the compass requires any corrections.

8. Worley was characterized by some as a "damned Dutchman." This was a World War I expression used to denote the German enemy by the Allies. Although naval records had shown Worley was born in San Francisco, later investigation proved that he was German-born and illegally entered the United States in 1878, when as a youth he deserted a German merchant ship in San Francisco. Extensive investigation by the navy after the *Cyclops* became overdue revealed that Worley was actually Johann Friedrich Georg Wichman. It was also brought out that whenever in port, even after he assumed command of the *Cyclops*, his closest male associates were German merchant ship captains. Could this combined with the fact that before the United States entered the war, Gottschalk was fanatically pro-German and a number

of the ship's crew were of German descent have any relation to the vessel's disappearance? When the loss of the ship was made public, many people, both civilian and military, conjectured that the vessel was handed over to the enemy. So strong was this sentiment that within hours after the armistice ending World War I was signed, Admiral William S. Sims, senior American naval officer in Europe, began investigating German naval files and records for any clue as to the fate of the *Cyclops*. It was ascertained that the *Cyclops* never reached Germany, and that there were no U-boats, surface raiders, or mines anywhere near where the big collier could have been steaming. However, a more thorough examination of the archives did reveal the name *Cyclops*. Far up in the North Atlantic, a U-boat commanded by a Lieutenant Doenitz, who would one day become Hitler's grand admiral, sank a British ship with all hands: *her name was Cyclops.*

Apparently, one can discount any treacherous act, for had the German High Command altered their naval records, some information would have had to leak out through the years. Had the prisoners and their cohorts successfully revolted and taken over the ship, where could they have gone? There are a considerable number of deep water areas in the South Atlantic where a scuttled ship could remain indefinitely undiscovered. But what about the mutineers? There are no islands or land masses in the adjacent waters remote enough to conceal the insurgents. Language barriers and skin color would have betrayed them. A minute handful, possibly four or five, might have made it passing off as beachcombers or explorers, but the chances of so small a band remaining out of over three hundred are unlikely.

National Marine and the *Literary Digest* have suggested the *Cyclops* plunged down into the deepest depths of the ocean while entwined in the tentacles of a giant octopus. This theory merits no mention other than the comment that Jules Verne's books were popular at the time.

In June, 1923, a group of naval and merchant officers in Baltimore, the *Cyclops's* destination, expressed the theory that the ship was sunk by her own cargo. A merchant ship officer, Captain Charles H. Zearfoss of the Munson Lines, was quoted as saying, "I think the *Cyclops* was sunk by her cargo. Manganese is a very difficult cargo to handle and the collier's crew was used to handling only coal. It has a tendency to settle down, grinding away whatever is below it. The *Cyclops* was not a 'tween deck ship and the cargo was loaded in the lower hold. I think the end came suddenly when the bottom practically dropped out." Captain Zearfoss's theory does merit some attention. But could the bottom drop out of all the ship's holds at one time? The odds of this occurring are almost nil.

Nervig suggested that as a result of Worley's improper loading of the cargo and his refusal to confer with his incarcerated executive officer that the cargo was unevenly distributed causing the ship to break in two and plummet to the bottom before anyone could get off. The heavy weight to bulk ratio of the cargo combined with the fact that the ship was known to be overloaded tends to support this theory. However, with the exception of submarines, few vessels have been built that would sink without anything aboard floating to the surface. And had the *Cyclops* actually broken in two, one end would have remained afloat long enough for some life rafts to be rigged or other wreckage to remain on the surface. Records show that with nearly every vessel that sank as a result of breaking in two, one half remained afloat long enough for some survivors to abandon ship.

Another oft-expressed theory is that the cargo, when being loaded, was improperly shored against shifting. In January, 1920, Lieutenant Commander Mahlon Tisdale, who had served on a number of navy colliers and even as communications officer aboard the *Cyclops* in 1916, stated, "Perhaps the cargo was braced to prevent shifting—but this would have required very strong braces, far beyond the capacity of the ship's carpenter. Unless these braces were installed at the loading port, they were probably not installed at all." Tisdale who also served on one of the *Cyclops*'s sister ships, the collier *Neptune,* went on, "I have seen the *Neptune* flop ten degrees for no apparent reason. If, in so flopping, something occurred to accentuate the list, is it not perfectly plausible to assume that this accentuation might have increased to such a degree as to cause the ship to turn turtle?" The behavior of manganese ore is such that once it starts moving or shifting the inertia caused by its weight will keep it moving until the original cause of the movement ceases. Thus, theoretically, the *Cyclops*'s cargo might have begun to shift and kept moving beyond the so-called point of no return. To continue with Tisdale's assumptions, "This could all occur in a few seconds and the ship would be bottom up before anyone could abandon ship. Some few men from the bridge and poop might have been thrown clear of the ship. But with everything secured for sea there would be little wreckage. Remember that there would be nothing adrift except such gear as would be free to float off during the few seconds during the turn [roll over]. There would be no debris such as always follows a sinking due to other marine casualty, as in the case of striking a mine or torpedo. There would have been no time for an SOS. There would have been no time for anything. The few men in the water could not have lived long of their own accord. Such small gear as did float off would have been lost in the vastness of the ocean long before the rescue vessels started their search." Lieutenant Commander Tisdale's reasoning is probably the most logical of any. But it, too, leaves room for debate. Certainly Worley would have had some shoring erected in the cargo holds even though it might have been inadequate. And it is possible that the bracings could have given way and started the cargo shifting under the strain created by the movement of the vessel, thus causing her to roll over bottom up. But again not all of the braces could have let go at once. There could have been a chain reaction, but not so quick that everyone aboard was taken off guard. The cargo was low in the holds—low enough that it would have taken more than "a few seconds" for it to shift far enough to cause the ship to capsize. There would have been time for at least one or two rafts or lifeboats to be readied and a radio signal transmitted.

Several months after the *Cyclops* was announced as lost, a bottle was found washed ashore not far from Atlantic City, New Jersey. In it was a note supposedly written in great haste as the *Cyclops* was going down. Obviously this message was a malevolent hoax. Had there been time aboard a sinking ship to locate a bottle, write a distress message, and seal it in the bottle, there would have been time to launch a boat and radio distress signals.

Some mention has been made of her ammunition lockers exploding, causing the *Cyclops* to sink. However, the fact that the ship was armed only with several three-inch deck guns would refute this possibility, for she would have carried insufficient explosives to be heavily damaged let alone sunk.

Weather was another much discussed probability. But any seas high enough to sink the *Cyclops* with all hands would surely have been noticed in other areas. Records show that there were heavy seas off the New England coast at the time the collier was lost, but this was well north of the *Cyclops*'s track. There are also reports of a cold front passing through the northern part of the West Indies about the time the *Cyclops* would have been passing that area, but the seas never reached such height as to instantly sink a vessel the size of the *Cyclops*.

As cited previously in analyzing Livingston's cable to the State Department, Worley was absolved by the government from any traitorous conspiracy with the Germans. However, in the September, 1923, issue of *Naval Institute Proceedings,* there is an almost obscure paragraph, a mentioning so vague and underplayed that it makes the reader wonder if there is more to it than meets the eye: "A ship built at Brunswick, Georgia, and said to have carried a number of spies, is known to have been seized off the Chesapeake about that time. At least one important person with strong German connections is known to have been on board the *Cyclops.*" There were only two important persons aboard the *Cyclops*—Gottschalk and Worley. Worley's German ties are known. What about the consul general? He was known to have been strongly pro-German before the war and of German ancestory.

One can come up with innumerable arguments one way or the other concerning the disappearance of the *Cyclops,* and every conjecture can be disputed with some logic. The only certainty is that somewhere in the "Devil's Triangle" the *Cyclops* vanished off the face of the earth without any trace whatsoever.

There are some interesting afterthoughts indirectly involving the *Cyclops*. In November, 1928, the liner *Vestris,* the same vessel that was the last to communicate with Worley's ship, was lost at sea with a heavy loss of life. She was on a course through the "Devil's Triangle" bound for Barbados, the *Cyclops's* last port of call.

Of the defendants in the murder case of Oscar Stewart aboard the *Pittsburgh,* only James Coker, the actual murderer, reached prison safely. When the *Cyclops* departed Brazilian waters with his three co-defendants, he remained aboard the *Pittsburgh* where he was to be hung. However, his sentence was commuted to life in prison. He eventually reached prison in New Hampshire where, ironically, after serving only three years he was ordered released by Secretary of the Navy Daniels.

Two of the *Cyclops's* sister ships, the colliers *Nereus* and *Proteus,* were taken out of service during the early 1920s and laid up at Norfolk Navy Yard until March, 1941, when they were sold as surplus to Saguenay Terminals, Ltd., of Ottawa as bulk carriers. The entry of the United States into World War II overshadowed any mention in the press of the fate that befell these two ships. On November 23, 1941, the *Proteus* sailed from Saint Thomas in the Virgin Islands with a cargo of bauxite bound for Norfolk. On December 10, the *Nereus* departed Saint Thomas also bound for Norfolk with a cargo of bauxite. Both of the *Cyclops's* sister ships entered the "Devil's Triangle" and vanished without a trace.

German naval archives were investigated at the termination of World War II for any clues as to the fate of the *Nereus* or the *Proteus*. The probe disclosed that at the time the two ships disappeared, there were no German U-boats, warships, or mines in or near the "Devil's Triangle." However, once again there was mention of the *Cyclops*. In January, 1941, off Cape Sable in the North Atlantic, a British ship was torpedoed and sunk, taking all ninety-four aboard down with her. The ship's name was *Cyclops*.

6. The Greatest Sailor
of Them All

Almost seventy years before Francis Chichester was knighted by the queen of England for sailing around the world alone, a retired American sea captain, Joshua Slocum, completed the first solo circumnavigation in a thirty-six-foot yawl, the *Spray* from Boston.

Sir Francis Chichester completed his voyage to fame at Plymouth, England, on May 18, 1967. Nine months earlier, on August 28, 1966, in his ketch *Gipsy Moth IV* this seagoing senior citizen began his 28,500-mile voyage from this same port a month before his sixty-fifth birthday. This old-age pensioner, who seven years before had been plagued with lung cancer, circumnavigated the globe in a vessel custom-built for the voyage. The venture was underwritten by several well-to-do backers. Sir Francis's boat was fifty-three-feet long, ten feet six inches across her beam, and drew seven feet nine inches of water.

The *Gipsy Moth IV*, whose master became sea sick every time he set out to sea, was equipped with the finest navigation devices including a worldwide

Marconi radio, wind speed and direction indicators, depth finder, radio direction finder, electric generator, a self-steering device, and even a beer dispenser. None the less, it was a most incredible feat considering the health and age of Chichester. In fact, there are only a handful of younger men in the world today who could achieve the same accomplishment. Sir Francis Chichester is considered the sailor of the century.

If Francis Chichester is the sailor of this century, then Joshua Slocum is without doubt the sailor of the last century. Many an old salt will give argument to anyone denying that Slocum is the greatest sailor of all time.

On April 24, 1895, two months after his fifty-first birthday, Joshua Slocum set sail from Boston on his single-handed voyage around the world, a distance of forty-six thousand miles. Chichester was attempting to equal the time set by the clipper ships; thus, he sailed the most direct routes and strived for all the speed that he could. On his three-year journey Slocum's only goal was to be the first man to sail around the globe alone. This accounts for the time and distance differences.

The *Spray*, measuring thirty-six feet nine inches in length, had a beam of fourteen feet two inches. Her draft was just over four feet. Not only was the *Spray* considerably smaller than the *Gipsy Moth IV*, but she was far less well equipped. When Slocum would cast off, he would have to do so either under sail or with the assistance of a towboat. Chichester merely cranked up his diesel auxiliary engine and headed out to wherever he wanted to hoist his sails.

The *Spray* emanated from a joke played on Slocum by a retired whaling captain. As the nineteenth century drew toward an end, steam was replacing sail as a means of nautical propulsion. Many of the tall sailing ships laid at dockside, their skeletal masts and yardarms stripped, waiting either for the ship breakers or for cargoes that would never come. Others had their masts removed and were towed about as coal barges. Hundreds of sailing-ship masters found themselves stranded on the beach or retired to "old sailors'" homes. Joshua Slocum, twenty-five years a sailing-ship captain, found himself beached. The ship owners no longer wanted the men who were instrumental in establishing the United States as one of the leading seafaring nations. Slocum spent his days browsing along the waterfronts, passing the time with watchmen aboard the laid-up sailing hulks, and talking with other unemployed captains. And it was one of these old cronies who offered Slocum a ship that "wants some repairs." The ship was located at Fairhaven just opposite New Bedford. The vessel was Slocum's for the taking—no strings attached.

The next day Slocum saw his "new" ship. He had been the butt of a hoax. For the *Spray* was an ancient wreck whose age none of the townsfolk could remember. She had been blocked up in a field several miles from the water for at least seven years. Being a resolute man and having little to do, Slocum accepted the prank as a challenge. The hulk required so much rebuilding that the many retired sea captains who visited with him during the eighteen months that he spent working on the boat couldn't tell whether the *Spray* was new or an old vessel rebuilt. Besides his labor Slocum spent $553.62 for materials with which to reincarnate the *Spray*.

The big question among those who knew the boat and the man was, Will it pay? The ship's sailing qualities were outstanding—the *Spray* had the ability and speed to outsail most other vessels anywhere near her size. It was only after an unsuccessful attempt at commercial fishing with the *Spray* that Slocum decided to sail her alone around the world. There were many critics of the old captain's plan, for the feat was considered impossible.

But Slocum was not a man to be deterred. And he embarked on the voyage, a voyage full of adventure, mystery, and close calls. In his book, *Sailing Alone Around the World,* Slocum describes an incident near the Azores in which he fell seriously ill. As he lay doubled up in pain on the floor of the boat's cabin a storm struck. But he was too sick and delirious to shorten sail. He passed out. Sometime later he awakened. The gale was still blowing. Looking out the companionway, he saw, to his astonishment, a man at the helm holding the *Spray* on a steady course in spite of the turbulence of the sea. The man was dressed in clothing of centuries past. The stranger introduced himself as being a member of Columbus's crew, the pilot of the *Pinta.* He said that he had come to guide Slocum's ship that night.

The next morning when Slocum had recovered sufficiently to go out on deck, the gale was moderating and the sun was shining. The strange helmsman was nowhere to be seen. Everything not secured had been washed away during the storm. The decks were whitened by the sunbaked salt spray. The gale had been more severe than Slocum had imagined. Yet, the sails that he had been too sick to furl were still set and pulling. They should have been ripped to shreds. Then he discovered that the *Spray* had made a good ninety miles right on course during the night. Only a helmsman could make that possible. Although unrecognized for years to come, this area is on the fringe of the "Devil's Triangle."

Slocum had originally plotted his course from west

to east—across the Atlantic, through the Mediterranean, Suez Canal, Red Sea, and into the Indian Ocean. Eventually he would cross the Pacific, round Cape Horn, and sail up the Atlantic back to Boston. But these plans were thwarted due to an attempted attack by Mediterranean pirates as he was approaching Gibraltar. The *Spray* proved its sailing qualities by outrunning the Arabs' dhow. Having been warned about the pirates in the Mediterranean and Red seas, Slocum after this encounter decided to head back across the Atlantic toward Cape Horn. His east to west circumnavigation included run-ins with savages, storms, self-esteemed customs officials, and the like. Because he lacked fifteen dollars to have his chronometer repaired, Slocum bought a tin one-dollar alarm clock with the minute hand missing and used this as his navigation timepiece. The only other navigation equipment aboard the *Spray* were a compass, a sextant, and sailing charts.

When Slocum sailed the *Spray* into the harbor of Boston on June 27, 1898, the fanfare was far less than that received by Chichester almost seventy years later. Only locally did the fifty-four-year-old sailor receive the honors he deserved, for the newspaper headlines were dominated by news of the Spanish-American War and the chain of American naval victories. Slocum's rise to fame was gradual as the war ended. But fame and glory did come to the old man and his old boat. His book not only became a best seller but also was required reading in public schools. And this sailor, who could not swim, was demanded worldwide as a lecturer.

In between his writing, public appearances, and other activities, Slocum still managed to find time to sail the *Spray*. In the autumns of 1905, 1907, and 1908, he set sail from his home at West Tisbury on

Martha's Vineyard, to spend those winters cruising alone through the West Indies.

In the fall of 1909, Slocum, then sixty-five years old, set forth on another single-handed voyage to the West Indies. On November 14, he put out to sea from Miami where he had stopped for supplies. Joshua Slocum, the greatest sailor of them all, and the *Spray* from Boston sailed into the "Devil's Triangle" and disappeared forever.

7. The Sulphur Ships

More incidents occurred in the "Devil's Triangle" in 1963 than in any other recent year. Ships, boats, planes, and yachts were victims. The most spectacular happened during the month of February. The mystery of the tanker *Marine Sulphur Queen* commenced when the tugboats pulled alongside and gently nudged her bow seaward toward the Gulf of Mexico for what was to be the last time on February 2, 1963. It was a routine operation for the chugging tugs. A few hundred feet to the stern was the pilot boat. It would follow the 523-foot T-2 tanker until she was clear of the ship channel and in the open sea. Then she would pull alongside the vessel and take off the pilot whose responsibility it was to guide the sulphur-laden tanker safely out of the harbor. The tugs would be required only to get the deeply loaded ship clear of the harbor and heading out through the ship channel with her $430,000 cargo.

The tanker's crew of thirty-nine had no apprehension as the lines from the tugboats were cast free that they would never reach their destination—Norfolk,

Virginia. The *Sulphur Queen* rode low enough in the water, as do most fully loaded tankers, that instead of using a Jacob's ladder to reach the pilot boat, the pilot simply stepped from the ship's well deck onto his boat, gave a farewell wave, and headed back to shore. The seven-thousand-ton tanker cleared her final port of call, Beaumont, Texas, and was now alone entering one of man's last unconquered realms—the open sea.

Once away from land, the usual shipboard routine began—securing loose gear, coiling and flaking lines, setting the bow watch, checking the compass, the routine radio check, regulating the steam valves of the vessel's turbine to give the ship the most practical speed. Off-duty men lounged at the fantail "chewing the gam," the sailors' term for gossiping. Her compass course was 135 degrees or about southeast.

Her cargo of molten sulphur was sustained at a temperature of 370 degrees Fahrenheit by live steam passing through steel heating coils supplied from the boiler room by insulated pipes running along the decks. The *Marine Sulphur Queen* had been converted from a wartime oil tanker. Basically, the conversion required little more than installing a means of maintaining the cargo at the correct temperature range—steam pipes, heating coils, and insulation chambers.

Nine years earlier in December, 1954, another sulphur-laden vessel, the *Southern Districts,* had been en route from Port Sulphur, Texas, to Bucksport, Maine. The ship was a 328-foot converted navy LST. She displaced thirty-three hundred tons. Built in 1944, she was one of the many such landing ships constructed in the Midwest and sailed down inland waterways to the Mississippi River and thence to the Gulf of Mexico. She had been built in Leaven-worth, Kansas, for the specific purpose of ramming ashore onto emeny beaches to off-load her cargo of tanks, trucks, jeeps, supplies, troops, and whatever else was needed to establish a beachhead. Her con-version from a wartime landing ship to a commercial bulk carrier required a number of modifications in-cluding the welding shut of her huge bow doors. She carried two thirty-man lifeboats.

The *Southern Districts* departed Port Sulphur on December 2, 1954. Her course was approximately identical to that of the *Marine Sulphur Queen*'s—southeast. Her two Fairbanks-Morse diesels pushed her along at a steady eight knots. After rounding the Florida Keys she changed to a northerly course up through the Straits of Florida. The Gulf Stream's three- to four-knot north-flowing current increased her speed over the bottom to eleven or twelve knots. She was carrying a crew of perhaps twenty-three men. The exact number is not known. The captain didn't leave a crew list before sailing as required. No less than three members of the crew walked off the ship just before she sailed. They had a feeling that she would never reach her destination as the vessel had been plagued by structural and steering problems.

Now the sulphur ship pushed on, transmitting a routine radio message. That was the last word heard from her. The *Southern Districts* simply vanished. The date was December 5, 1954—exactly nine years to the day after the six navy planes disappeared over the same area. The navy and coast guard searched over 262,000 square miles, but nothing from the ship was recovered. Again history had repeated itself. For on January 20, 1921, another sulphur ship, the *Hewitt*, sailed from Sabine Pass, Texas, bound for Boston. The Union Sulphur Company vessel rounded the Florida

Keys, entered the Straits of Florida, communicated with another vessel north of Jupiter Island, Florida, and vanished. The *Hewitt* was one of at least ten ships that disappeared in the western Atlantic in the space of a few months early in 1921.

As the 16,500-ton *Marine Sulphur Queen* rounded the Florida Keys, a crew member sent a radiogram to his wife telling her of the expected arrival time in Norfolk. Another crewman sent a radio message to his stockbroker in Tampa. Nothing else was ever heard from the *Marine Sulphur Queen*. She entered the Straits of Florida, very near where the *Southern Districts* had nine years earlier, and vanished. She, too, had voyaged into the "Devil's Triangle."

On February 6, she was reported as overdue. Coast guard bases from Key West to Norfolk dispatched aircraft and surface vessels in a systematic search extending from the eastern Gulf of Mexico to beyond the Virginia capes and as far east as Bermuda. Every object from similar-looking T-2 tankers to masses of yellow seaweed resembling floating sulphur from the air was investigated. Some life jackets were found off the Florida Keys, but they were never proved to have been from the missing tanker.

In June, 1969, a deposition hearing was held in New York to determine whether or not the ship's owners, Marine Transport Lines of New York, were negligent and liable for claims filed by the families of the lost crew members. The owners brought in a retired sea captain, seventy-two-year-old George H. Grant of Surf City, New Jersey. Grant, who in forty-seven years at sea made over a thousand trips through the area where the *Marine Sulphur Queen* was believed lost, theorized that the tanker "encountered extremely high seas known to sailors as a 'freak sea' and . . . rolled over and sank." Upon cross-examination Grant conceded that he never met "freak seas" in the area or heard of other ships sunk by them. The claimants' lawyer, Donald E. Klein, brought in a meteorologist-oceanographer who disputed Captain Grant's theory.

William Donn, professor and director of Columbia University's Atmospheric Science Laboratory, was asked by Klein, "Were the conditions in or near the Straits of Florida such that a confused sea, or an interference sea, or a freak sea, or a freak wave could have been generated?"

"No, sir," Donn replied.

"Was there anything unusual about the weather and sea conditions in the Gulf of Mexico and the Straits of Florida during the month of February, 1963?" Klein asked.

"No, sir," Donn said. "I would say that the kind of weather prevailing there on the days in question was expectable, on the basis of past weather behavior."

A coast guard report showed that at least ten T-2 tankers had broken in two and sunk resulting in an order for all existing T-2 tankers to have a steel reinforcement belt added around the hull at the waterline.

But did the *Marine Sulphur Queen* go down? Another theory is that she went up. A coast guard report issued in April, 1964, was critical of the ship's owners on two counts: failure to follow good operating practice by not giving instructions or assistance to the ship's master on many aspects of the problems of transporting molten sulphur; and failure to keep itself informed as to matters affecting the vessel's safety. Investigation by the coast guard revealed that on earlier voyages a number of fires had occurred in the sulphur-impregnated insulation in the void spaces around the tanks.

Could fire have broken out again aboard the *Marine Sulphur Queen*? Could a panic situation have ensued at the thought of fighting fire and a possible explosion at sea? Could those who attempted to fight the fire have become overwhelmed by the toxic sulphur fumes? Sulphur fumes that could have permeated throughout the vessel by way of the air ducts and ventilators overcoming all hands including the radio operator even before a distress signal could be transmitted? Could the *Marine Sulphur Queen* have become so full of sulphur fumes that she became a floating bomb? Could cold seawater somehow have come in contact with the 370-degree molten sulphur and caused an explosion so violent that the ship was virtually ripped to pieces?

Although seven life jackets and other items that could have come from the ill-fated ship were never officially authenticated, there is one clue that supports the theory that the ship was engulfed by a shattering explosion—a blast that disintegrated the *Marine Sulphur Queen* in an instant. Shortly after the tanker was listed as missing, Miami boat builder John Allmand and his small son were driftwood hunting along the beach on Key Biscayne, Florida, almost within sight of President Nixon's winter White House. "We saw what appeared to be part of a diving board being tossed about in the surf about fifty feet from shore. So my son and I waded out and dragged it onto the beach. Both ends were splintered or shattered, so we turned the board over and saw that it was black with white letters 'ARINE SULPH' painted on it. The board which was about twelve inches wide by about seven feet long had broken bolts sticking through it as though it had been secured to something." What John Allmand and his son found was what was left of the missing ship's trail board. (A trail board is a sign on either side of a ship's bridge giving the vessel's name.) From the appearance of the splintered trail board one can only conclude that the *Marine Sulphur Queen* was ripped apart by a savage explosion—quite possibly touched off by a chemical reaction resulting from cold seawater coming in contact with hot bubbling sulphur.

Almost without exception, every article or story written about the "Devil's Triangle," the "Bermuda Triangle," the "Twilight Zone of the Atlantic," or any other name one wants to use to refer to the area, includes the loss of the *Marine Sulphur Queen* as a strange mystery. There was nothing mysterious or supernatural—simply an industrial explosion at sea.

Without doubt, some readers will disagree with this explanation of what happened to the *Marine Sulphur Queen,* and for their information, another tragic occurrence will be reported.

On February 2, 1972, exactly nine years to the day that the *Marine Sulphur Queen* began her last voyage, another T-2 tanker, the *V. A. Fogg,* vanished in the Gulf of Mexico just after her departure from Freeport, Texas. And like the *Marine Sulphur Queen,* the *V. A. Fogg* carried exactly thirty-nine men when she disappeared. However, she was missing in water averaging less than 150 feet in depth.

Had it been the "Devil's Triangle" and not the Gulf of Mexico where the *V. A. Fogg* was lost, she would certainly have been listed as another strange disappearance. The UFO researchers would have brought out their theories, the occultists would attribute the occurrence to a "space warp" or "Atlanteans from another dimension," and others would blame Martians with magnetic ray guns. But the *V. A. Fogg* would be the subject of many future stories about the "triangle"—same type ship, same number in crew, same day exactly nine years later, etc.

Yes, there are more than an average number of similarities between the two disappearances. But there are a number of differences too. The *V. A. Fogg* was missing in waters less than 150 feet deep rather than in the many thousand-foot depths of the "Devil's Triangle." Her voyage was to last but thirteen hours as her destination was Houston. She would have carried forty men, but one crewman, John Caldira, Jr., of Galveston, missed the ship after being caught in a traffic jam while driving to the port. Shortly after the vessel left port, a Space Agency pilot reported seeing a column of black smoke ten thousand feet in the air over the ship's route. Three coast guard cutters, the *Valiant, Gentian,* and *Reliance,* along with a dozen airplanes and helicopters and a number of private vessels searched a twenty-thousand-square-mile area. Rough seas and fifty-mile-an-hour winds hampered the search. At times conditions became so difficult that planes and helicopters flying at five-hundred feet had no vision because of salt spray building up on their windshields. After eleven days, the search was called off. Then Joseph Cheavens, an attorney for the *V. A. Fogg*'s owners, checked the tape recording between the Space Agency pilot and the control tower. Through a communications error the coast guard had been searching miles from where the column of black smoke had been seen.

The company chartered a research vessel equipped with side-scanning radar and special sonar gear and had it search an area pinpointed by Cheavens, and within eleven hours the wreck was found. On February 14, divers went down to the ship and brought up the vessel's trail board. Later underwater photographs were taken showing buckled and twisted one-inch steel plates, hatches blown away, the sides of the hull crumpled, gapping seams, and tanks that had been filled with benzene vapors having exploded in a domino fashion "blowing up," one diver said, "like a string of firecrackers." It was obvious that the *V. A. Fogg* had exploded and sunk within seconds. A number of bodies, including that of her captain, John Christie, were recovered.

But suppose the tanker had gone down under the same circumstances in the Atlantic Ocean rather than in the Gulf of Mexico. She was fifty miles offshore as required by law because she had been transporting highly toxic and extremely explosive benzene. Residue still remained in her tanks, and during the removal of the residue, she had to remain that distance offshore. Off the east coast of Florida, Georgia, or the Carolinas that distance would have placed her well into the "triangle." She would be resting in thousands of feet of water—rather than in the ninety feet where she was found—beyond the reach of divers or most sonar scanning devices. And if no one was flying over the area at the time the ten-thousand-foot-high column of smoke was still visible, she would be listed as having disappeared without a trace in the "Devil's Triangle."

How many of the "triangle's" victims did actually disappear for reasons other than human error, mechanical malfunction, structural failure, or weather phenomenon? Is there really a mystery out there, or is it just that explainable tragedies happened at a time when no witnesses were present and the few clues, if any, that might have remained were swept out into the vastness of the empty ocean before search and rescue vessels arrived at the scene?

8. The Christmastime Hex

It is the season to be jolly; it is a time of joy and merriment—every place, that is, except in the "Devil's Triangle." An unusual number of strange occurrences take place in the "triangle" during the Christmas season. We already know of the baffling mystery of the navy planes from Fort Lauderdale Naval Air Station that "never returned" just a few short weeks before Christmas, 1945. But there are other happenings, not as spectacular, but just as peculiar. They are mentioned throughout this book, but this chapter is devoted to three directly associated with the holiday season.

Shortly after dusk on December 27, 1948, as the mist left from late-afternoon showers rolled down into San Juan from the surrounding hills, a chartered DC-3 airliner climbed skyward and assumed a course of west north west leaving the glow of lights from Puerto Rico's capital city behind. The plane's destination was Miami some 1,150 miles distant. Her three-member crew consisted of pilot Robert Linquist of

Fort Myers, Florida, copilot Ernest Hill, Jr., of Miami, and stewardess Mary Burke of Newark, New Jersey. The twenty-nine passengers, mostly in their twenties and including two babies, were predominantly from New York City.

They had been spending the Christmas holidays with friends and relatives in their native country. Even though they were leaving the warmth and sunshine of the land of their origin to return to the raw, cold, windswept concrete canyons of Manhattan, the spirit of Christmas prevailed in the plane's cabin. It had been a good Yuletide. After serving a snack of coffee and cookies and seeing to the two mothers nursing their infants, stewardess Burke dimmed the cabin lights. Most of the passengers dozed off to sleep. Some, however, preferred to continue to celebrate until their bottles of Puerto Rican rum ran dry. The cockpit crew switched radio frequency from San Juan to Miami.

The DC-3, although not a large plane, is considered one of the most reliable aircraft ever built. It is the civilian version of the military's C-47 twin-engined craft that was so widely used during World War II. Today, in the 1970s, many DC-3s built during the 1940s are still in regular use employed at everything from hauling supplies and personnel to and from remote jungle mining camps to conveying prospective home buyers on sightseeing flights to real estate developments. And if parts remain available, they'll probably still be in service well into the 1980s.

The smoothly purring engines of Captain Linquist's plane droned steadfastly on hour after hour. Shortly after midnight she was winging over the Caicos Islands in the southeastern Bahama Islands and would soon be making the transition from Atlantic to Eastern Standard time.

The excursionists were awakened by the pilot shortly after 4 A.M. and informed that they would soon be landing in Miami for customs inspection, fuel, and a fresh crew before proceeding on to New York. With the brightening of the cabin lights, the passengers began gathering up their carry-aboard belongings in preparation for debarkation at the Miami customs building. Joy and merriment still filled the cabin for a number of celebrants were singing Christmas carols in Spanish.

At 4:13 A.M. the Miami tower operator heard from Captain Linquist that all was well. Behind the pilot's voice could be heard the carolers, almost as though there was recorded background music. "We're fifty miles south of the field . . . can see the glow from Miami's lights. Am standing by for landing instructions." The tower operator received no response to his reply. Over and over he tried to reestablish contact with the DC-3 but to no avail.

With the first gray of dawn two hours later, a search was already under way—an operation that would later consist of no less than fifty planes and ten ships and a dozen small boats. The last estimated position of the missing plane was in the vicinity of Key Largo, over fifteen to twenty feet of water with a white sand bottom. In water that shallow wreckage could easily be spotted from the air even were the craft to have disintegrated upon impact. But no trace of the DC-3 or its occupants was ever found by the searchers. On January 10, Airborne Transport, the plane's lessee, announced jointly with the coast guard that the search had been terminated.

Several days later a beachcomber named Voss found several labelless bottles partially filled with Puerto Rican rum washed ashore on Miami Beach. By the time word of this discovery reached the authorities, the finder had already consumed the contents of the bottles . . . thus eliminating forever what may have been the only clues to the fate of the joyous but doomed Christmastime flight of the DC-3 and all thirty-two aboard.

Yes, it is a time for joy and merriment, and that is the way forty-two-year-old Dan Burrack, a Miami Beach hotel owner, and Father Patrick Horgan, thirty-five, a priest from Saint George's Catholic Church in Fort Lauderdale, felt as they cast off the lines from Burrack's twenty-three-foot white twin-engined Chris Craft cabin cruiser. As the boat worked its way through the maze of canals surrounding Burrack's island home in one of Miami Beach's most fashionable neighborhoods, they commented on the decorative Christmas lights being turned on along their route toward the ocean. It was 8 P.M., Friday, December 22, 1967—the first day of winter. A cold front was moving toward Miami from the northwest. However, the concrete wall of hotels and the east-facing Miami Beach shoreline provided good protection from the increasing winds.

At 8:30 P.M. they cleared Government Cut, the inlet leading from Miami harbor to the ocean. Revving both engines to near full throttle the two men headed seaward to behold the Christmas lights of Miami Beach from a mile out at sea—a mile that was to stretch into infinity.

At 9 P.M., Miami Beach coast guard received a radio message from Burrack that his boat had become disabled after the propellers of his outdrives had struck a submerged object. However, he reported, the boat was taking on no water.

At 9:03 P.M. a coast guard crew in a forty-foot cutter was on its way to assist. Here were men who knew these waters like the backs of their hands. They were professionals fully trained in every phase of search and rescue.

Meanwhile, Burrack and Father Horgan, knowing that their boat was unsinkable due to built-in flotation chambers and that the coast guard was en route, had little to do but watch the lights from the vicinity of buoy number 7 one mile off Miami Beach.

Unaware that they'd be spending their Christmas searching for a missing boat, the coast guard crew reached the location given by Burrack only eighteen minutes after his original call. But they found only the buoy marking the ship channel into the harbor and increasing seas. There was no sign of the disabled craft or its occupants.

A search was conducted from the Florida Keys to Jacksonville and 150 miles out to sea. Even though the missing boat was last heard from in an area lit by the lights of Miami Beach, she was still in the "Devil's Triangle."

After being fully cooperative with the press throughout the first five days of the search, the coast guard suddenly refused to release any information as to exactly what was radioed by Burrack during his first and only message. A coast guard spokesman said only that Burrack sounded like he was in an "unusual" situation. A coast guard legal officer said they were not at liberty to divulge the information.

Friends of Burrack stated that although he was not a "blue water–rough seas" sailor, he was fully capable of handling his boat and had it equipped with every safety device available for a craft of its size. After the search was called off, a coast guard spokesman said, "We presume they are missing, but not lost at sea." And "missing" they were: Father Patrick Horgan, Dan Burrack, and a twenty-three-foot cabin cruiser that lived up to its name—*Witchcraft!*

Traditionally, breaking a bottle of champagne against the bow of a new vessel as it is about to be launched assures her of good luck and fair sailing. It was a gala occasion when publisher Harvey Conover launched his sleek new yawl *Revonoc* (Conover spelled backward) at Mamaroneck, New York, in 1956. The event was attended by sailing enthusiasts from all parts of New England, for *Revonoc* was to be the boat to beat during the upcoming racing season. She was designed for racing on the high seas in all weather. And unlike Dan Burrack, Harvey Conover was considered one of the most experienced and able "blue water" sailors on the entire eastern seaboard. Few yachtsmen could match him in sailing ability and seamanship.

After a summer of successful racing competition in her home waters, the *Revonoc* was sailed to Florida where she was taking on all comers in the offshore racing circuit. Yes, she was the boat to beat. During the week before Christmas, the Conovers enjoyed a relaxing cruise down through the Florida Keys.

After spending a joyous Christmas in Key West, Harvey Conover, his wife, daughter, and son-in-law set sail for Miami, which was 150 miles to the north —a course on which they'd always be within sight of land. But, nevertheless, it was still 150 miles through the "Devil's Triangle." Before the Cuban weather stations went off the air, as they usually did at dark each night, they gave a marine weather report that forecast good weather.

The Conovers experienced fair sailing until they were just south of Miami where they encountered a sudden change in wind direction from southeast to north. A violent cold front had slammed in on them. But Conover was an able sailor and *Revonoc* was a staunch vessel. Weather such as this was nothing new to either the man or his boat. And besides, there was to be a gala New Year's celebration at the yacht club that evening.

The year 1957 was blasted out by the howling norther that came roaring down through the Straits of Florida. *Revonoc* plunged onward, for she was only a few short miles from shelter. As the gusting winds exploded across Miami's Biscayne Bay, they carried with them strains of "Auld Lang Syne," for the Conovers' friends reveling at the club were unaware that one of their sailing buddies and his ship were fighting for life just a few miles away.

When that first tumultous dawn of 1958 broke, *Revonoc* was no more. She had vanished. A search for the missing yacht was immediately undertaken by the coast guard and navy. As word spread to the Conovers' many friends they too joined the search—some even risking their own yachts and personal safety. All that was ever found was the yawl's undamaged eight-foot dinghy washed ashore at Hillsboro Lighthouse some forty miles north of Miami.

Another yachtsman of world renown is Richard Bertram who participated in the search for *Revonoc* and was a close family friend of the Conovers. Bertram refuses to believe that Conover and the *Revonoc* succumbed to the sea and weather. "Harvey Conover was too good a sailor to let that happen to him," said Bertram. He thinks that the missing yawl was most likely run down by a ship and ground to pieces by the churning propeller(s). This is a possibility for several reasons. There is an almost steady stream of southbound ships hugging the Florida coastline to avoid the northward push of the Gulf Stream, which is virtually a river within the sea. With the advent of highly sophisticated radar, many vessels no longer maintain a bow watch, and a wooden boat such as *Revonoc* in very turbulent seas would be difficult to detect on a radar screen. Also, many vessels, particularly those of foreign registry, lack the personnel to operate radar under all conditions. A fully loaded ship, such as a tanker, could run down even a large yacht, and the ship's crew wouldn't even feel it especially if the vessel were already rising and falling with large seas. There are numerous documented incidents of ships smashing into small craft and continuing on their way completely oblivious that an accident had occurred. Could this have happened to the *Revonoc*? If so, why did the little eight-foot dinghy survive?

When the subject of UFOs and "time" or "space warps" was brought up, Bertram, who has participated in every offshore ocean race in the world, commented, "Many people, when confronted with a situation that they don't understand, tend to attribute it to the supernatural. But I am sure that some day there will be found a logical and scientific explanation for all of these occurrences."

Could *Revonoc* have been run down by a ship in the night? Possibly, but what about Captain Linquist's DC-3, which vanished over water only twenty to thirty feet deep? Could the pilot have miscalculated his position and have been but a few miles to the east—a few miles farther out where the water's depth ranges to thousands of feet? This is the most logical explanation for the loss of the DC-3 if one believes in logic rather than the supernatural. But then, what about the loss of the *Witchcraft*? Could the craft have been blown seaward by the rising winds even as the coast guard cutter was heading out to her original position? There was a radio aboard, but possibly the *Witchcraft* actually was taking on water and her batteries flooded out, putting the radio out of commission. Also if Burrack was as experienced and his boat as well equipped as his friends stated, why didn't he anchor, for his original position was in water varying between thirty and forty feet deep? Then too the boat was "unsinkable" due to the built-in flotation chambers.

But what about the coast guard spokesman who, five days after the search was under way, suddenly refused to comment on Burrack's distress message other than that he sounded like he was in an "unusual" situation? Burrack's last words, or at least the last ones that the coast guard released, were, "It's pretty odd. I've never seen one like this!" It seems that twenty-two years earlier to the month five navy planes were also in an "unusual" situation.

9. On The Beach

Fort Lauderdale is the mecca of college students from all over the eastern half of the United States each spring. The beach here is one of the finest and safest on Florida's Gold Coast. For three miles there is no concrete wall of hotels and high-rise apartment buildings obstructing public access to the beach as is so common to other Florida cities along the Atlantic Ocean. And unlike other Florida cities, it is not a haven for senior citizens, but where the young crowd goes. There is little undertow to endanger swimmers. Large waves are rare except during inclement weather. The Bahama Islands, half a hundred miles to the east, form a natural barrier against the long Atlantic swells. Potentially, the most dangerous aspect of this beach is pollution caused by ocean-sewage outfall originating off Miami Beach and Hollywood to the south being carried north by the Gulf Stream's current.

It is over this beach that a number of airplanes, including those of the ill-fated Flight 19, have flown off into oblivion. It is past this beach that dozens of

outward-bound ships and yachts have voyaged to unknown watery graves. And it is at this beach that
one can walk to the water's edge, put one foot in the
ocean, look out to sea, and say, "Now, I have one
foot in the 'Devil's Triangle.'"

At 2:30 on the afternoon of June 19, 1972, a 1964
white Chevrolet Impala convertible pulled off Sun-
rise Boulevard, one of Fort Lauderdale's main
thoroughfares, into a parking space on Highway A1A,
which runs parallel to the ocean. The top was down,
and sticking out of the back was an eight-foot sailing
dinghy. Seventeen-year-old Tom Robinson of Fort
Lauderdale was taking his girl friend, Cathy Wheeler,
also seventeen, for an afternoon sail. They left their
billfolds, shoes, Cathy's glasses, and other personal
things locked in the glove compartment. The two
teenagers, dressed in T-shirts and cutoff blue jeans,
lugged the red-and-white boat down to the water's
edge. As they shoved off from shore, they must have
been the envy of those who had to be content with
lying in the sand or frolicking in the gentle surf at
one of the most crowded sections of Fort Lauderdale's
beach. Tom and Cathy had everything going for
them. They had just graduated from Stanahan High
School and both had been accepted for college in the
fall. They were young and had the whole world before them.

It was 3 P.M. when they stepped the mast, raised
the small boat's sail, and wove their way through
dozens of bathers relaxing in the clear warm waters.
Their plans were to stay but a few hundred feet from
shore tacking the boat along parallel to the beach. A
gentle wind was blowing from the west. Only a few
scattered clouds were in the sky. The sun was still
high above Schrafft's Hotel across the street. They
were seen laughing and having a good time —less

than a hundred yards from shore. That was the last that was ever seen of Catherine Ann Wheeler, honor student, and Thomas Robinson, high-school football player, and their little red-and-white sailboat. For as close to shore as they were, they were already in the "Devil's Triangle."

When they failed to return home that night, Tom's parents went down to the beach and found the white car just where Tom had left it. The personal belongings were still in it. The next morning a search and rescue operation commenced, or rather was expanded. For this made three boats that the coast guard was looking for. Eighteen-year-old Steven Whithurst of West Palm Beach was missing in his eighteen-foot motorboat, *Doc's Order*. Also missing was a thirty-five-foot sailboat carrying six young men, a girl, and a dog. The latter was poorly rigged, carried no name or numbers, and the crew was completely unfamiliar with even the basic fundamentals of sailing. They were last seen struggling through trial and error to raise the sails as the boat moved north in the Gulf Stream—sideways.

Two days later the Greek ship *Delphic Eagle* found young Steven Whithurst adrift 140 miles east of Saint Augustine—over 300 miles from where he was last seen, but still safe and sound. Soon after this, the thirty-five-foot sailboat with its neophyte crew was found tied to an abandoned dock not far from where the attempted cruise had originated. But Tom Robinson and Cathy Wheeler were still missing.

The coast guard search covered an area larger than the states of Vermont, Rhode Island, and New Hampshire combined. Lieutenant D. C. Hibbard and Lieutenant Commander H. C. McKean had just returned from a ten-hour search mission covering over fourteen-hundred square miles in the area between

Palm Beach and Grand Bahama Island. They were relaxing at the base officers' club. As Hibbard poured his beer into a glass, he commented, "There are two kids out there, and we haven't found them. We've searched every inch of that water. And when you can't find those kids, and you know they're in a tight situation, it really gets to you."

At dawn the next day, the two officers and their crew of six were aloft again searching a different grid section in their Albatross amphibian. They were flying at 750 feet with a cruising speed of 125 miles per hour. Two observers secured by safety belts were leaning out of the back doors. They would observe for one hour and be relieved for one hour alternately with another pair of observers. Thus, the pilot, co-pilot, and two observers were continuously scanning the waters beneath the plane as were the crews of five other planes, three helicopters, and a number of surface vessels. Catherine's father had joined the search in a friend's private aircraft. The waters were clear and calm. The search lasted for days, but no trace of the little red-and-white boat or its two young occupants was ever found.

Pompano Beach is the next city north of Fort Lauderdale. It is known for its harness-racing track, its lighthouse at Hillsboro Inlet, and a municipal fishing pier that extends several hundred yards out into the Atlantic Ocean. On Monday, December 29, 1969, throngs of schoolchildren were at the beach as it was Christmas vacation and school was out. Two schoolmates from Parkview Elementary School, nine-year-old Peggy Rahn and eight-year-old Wendy Stevenson met at the seashore. They attempted to go out onto the municipal fishing pier but were turned away as too young to venture out unsupervised. Blonde Peggy and dark-haired Wendy, clad only in their bathing suits, were seen walking away from the pier along the beach. They were never heard from or seen again. Police discounted the possibility that they ventured into the water at the beach and were drowned because no bodies were ever found. What happened to those two little girls is a mystery. Nevertheless, they were at the edge of the "Devil's Triangle."

Acklins Island in the Bahamas is one of those places that has yet to succumb to the rapacity of the developers and tourism. It is several hundred miles southeast of Nassau and is probably best known for the Castle Island lighthouse located near the south end of the island. This most important light in the West Indies, due to the magnitude of ship traffic that passes it, is best described as being a 135-foot-high red-and-white barber pole. The geographic names of the various parts of the island are intriguing: Bob's Nose, Snug Corner, Burial Ground Cay, and Delectable Bay. The island is an ideal place to live if one wants to raise his family away from the evils of civilization.

On August 14, 1971, four small boys all under ten years of age, the three Rolles brothers and Derrick Hanna, found an old wooden skiff lying on the beach. It had been reposing there for over two years, "and, therefore, was not exactly watertight," said an island official. The boys shoved, pulled, and tugged the old boat into the quiet waters of Delectable Bay and proceeded to play sailor. After all, their fathers earned their livelihoods from the sea. And what could be more fun for small boys on a summer Saturday afternoon. Whether there were any witnesses to what happened is unknown, but the old wooden skiff with its crew of four little boys vanished.

In 1851, the Great Exposition of London was held in that city's Hyde Park. The event was the nineteenth-century equivalent to the world's fairs and expos of modern times. The major building at the Great Exposition was an iron structure that reached 152 feet into the air. Fairgoers from all of England came to see and climb the great tower. The structure remained for several years after the other exhibits had been removed. Then one day workmen began to carefully dismantle the lofty edifice. Piece by piece the daring ironworkers unrigged the tower. As each section was removed, it was code marked in order that it might be reassembled with a minimum of difficulty. Shortly after the disassembly was completed, the pieces of what had become a huge iron jigsaw puzzle were loaded onto wagons and delivered to several Thames River wharves. Next they were lowered into the holds of three ships that were towed down the river to the sea. Soon they were en route across the Atlantic.

Great Isaacs Rock is located on the western fringes of the Bahama Islands some twenty miles north of Bimini and fifty-five miles east of Fort Lauderdale. At its longest point it measures but three-quarters of a mile. The surrounding waters abound with jagged coral reefs. And it was to this rock that the dismantled sections of the former Hyde Park landmark were delivered in 1859. Most of the same workers who had disassembled the tower reassembled it. While the construction was going on, there occurred a spectural phenomena that made most of the workers want to abandon the project and leave the island rock. They had seen the ghost of the "Gray Lady." Many years before, during a gale, a British square-rigger was dashed to pieces on the reefs just off the rock. There was but one survivor—a tiny infant. The child was washed onto Great Isaacs Rock where salvagers found the baby several days afterward. The baby, none the worse for the experience, was taken to Bimini Island and eventually returned to relatives in England. According to local natives this was only the beginning of the story. Just before each full moon the ghost of the baby's mother, who perished in the wreck, would walk the length of Great Isaacs Rock weeping for her child.

In as much as the ships were gone and radios hadn't been invented, a persuasive construction captain managed to get the structure erected. Upon completion of the reassembly job, a powerful light was installed atop the 152-foot tower, and red-and-white stripes were painted around the new lighthouse, which was named Victoria Light in honor of the empire's queen. Today it is known as Great Isaacs Light. The erection crew left, and the lighthouse keepers took over.

"The Gray Lady of Great Isaacs Light," as the spirit was called, continued her regular visits several nights before each full moon. A number of keepers resigned from their jobs after one month on the island rock. The ghostly visits went on until after the turn of the century. Finally, one night, a zealous head lightkeeper, who was also a layman of the church, performed a religious rite along the Gray Lady's path that convinced her that her child was safe. She never returned—so goes the story. But there are those who still swear that on dark stormy nights between three-quarters and full moon, the wailing voice of a woman can be heard on Great Isaacs Rock.

Down through the years, the towering structure that was the pride of the 1851 Great Exposition of London was unheralded by the world except for passing mariners and the men who kept its light burning. That is until August 4, 1969, when two of the lighthouse's keepers Ivan Major and B. Mollings simply vanished never to be seen again.

A Miami fisherman, Bruce Mounier, claims that shortly after the incident, he was in his small boat within sight of Great Isaacs Light when he saw what he believed to be two underwater UFOs—large gray egg-shaped objects about sixty feet long moving through the water at a high rate of speed just below the surface.

Daytona Beach, Florida, is known as the "Speed Capitol of the World." For it is here and at Ormond Beach, "The Birthplace of Speed," several miles to the north, that more automobile speed records have been broken than any other place. The actual beach is composed of hard, solidly packed grains of sand that provide exceptional traction and support for high-performance automobiles. Until Daytona Beach became a resort center in the late 1930s, the beach was considered to be the world's longest natural drag strip. Even today, bathers and sun worshipers drive and park their cars on the beach just above the high-tide mark.

During the month of February, 1935, Sir Malcolm Campbell was testing his racing car, the Blue Bird Special, on the beach at Daytona. For miles around the ear-splitting "vaarrroooom" of the vehicle could be heard as it neared three hundred miles per hour. People would line the balconies of the oceanfront hotels watching the fastest man on land roaring past in the world's fastest automobile.

Among the hundreds of tourists visiting Daytona Beach at that time were Atlanta furniture manufacturer Forrest Additon and his wife Bessie. For the couple it was a combined winter vacation and celebration of Bessie's birthday. On Friday, February 27, they spent the afternoon on the balcony outside their room at the Hotel Daytona Beach watching the Blue Bird Special making its record-breaking runs along the beach.

About seven that evening the Additons celebrated Bessie's birthday in the hotel's dining room. Sitting at the next table was Sir Malcolm himself, who wished Mrs. Additon a happy birthday by autographing her menu. After dinner the Atlanta couple went to the beach to watch the sea at night, for Bessie had never seen the ocean before this trip. The lights from the hotels cast a glow hundreds of feet onto the sea. With the exception of a chill resulting from an approaching cold front, it was a clear, beautiful night. The gleam of the lights from shore danced on the wave crests. All was quiet except for the slow gentle roar of the surf, a stark contrast to the thunder of the screaming cars that raced up and down the beach during the day. Hundreds of people were walking along the beach that night.

Shortly before 10 P.M. the Additons decided to retire to their fourth-floor room that overlooked the ocean. As Mrs. Additon recalled, "My husband went to the window to draw the shade. All of a sudden this plane came in, and my husband shouted, 'It looks like it's coming right through our window!' and he had hardly gotten the words out of his mouth when the plane went right down into the sea. In what seemed like just a few minutes, the coast guard was out . . . a number of them . . . all these boats were out and the searchlights were on, and I never saw the ocean so beautiful. You could see every detail everywhere from all of those bright lights. And they searched all night long, and they never found a single trace of that airplane."

Contact was made with every airport in Florida and Georgia to check on any missing planes or pilots. The results indicated no missing or overdue airplanes. Several days later, local newspaper headlines read: "Plane Disaster Rumor Appears Without Basis." The press went on to say that coast guard headquarters in Jacksonville discounted the rumors as erroneous because no wreckage was found. But were the rumors erroneous? And were they only rumors? Hundreds of people saw the plane go down. It hit less than a hundred yards from shore. The water was too shallow for any current to carry the wreckage away. The description of the craft by various witnesses matched —a silvery plane with red-and-green wing-tip lights. The witnesses were mostly people who had not known each other, and many never saw each other until an instant after the crash. Could hundreds of people have imagined what they saw? What was the phantom object that Bessie and Forrest Additon thought was going to crash into their hotel window? Could it have been some form of apparition? An aerial version of the legendary "Flying Dutchman"? Whatever it was, it appeared in the "Devil's Triangle."

Only a firm believer in the occult would claim dogmatically that these mysteries that occurred on or near the beach were the results of strange or supernatural forces. It is well within the realm of possibility that Tom Robinson and Cathy Wheeler were blown out to sea in their little sailboat by the west wind that prevailed that day. While they were cruising near the shore, protected from the offshore wind by the tall buildings across the street from the beach, things went fine. But once out of the lee of those buildings, the wind became more than their eight-foot dinghy could withstand. Thus they were carried out to sea. When a west wind blows across the Straits of Florida, the Gulf Stream is pushed from the Florida coast eastward and compressed against the Bahama Banks. The same amount of water flows north with the Gulf Stream but at a greater velocity, meaning that what might be a maximum current of four knots at the axis of this river in the sea could actually increase to over six nautical miles per hour.

Once Tom and Cathy were out in the Gulf Stream, they could have been carried as much as one hundred miles to the north and far to the east out into the open Atlantic before the search ever got under way. And if their sail or mast were damaged, they would have drifted on and on helplessly. This is a busy shipping lane where there is a possibility of a drifting boat being sighted by a passing ship, but there is also a possibility that such a boat could have been run down by a ship during the night. Had the wreckage floated, it would have been difficult to spot the hull, which was more white than red among the whitecaps of the waves.

A number of possibilities have been offered to explain the tragic fate of the two little girls from Pompano Beach, Peggy Rahn and Wendy Stevenson: drowning, sharks, a sex deviate, kidnapping.

The four little boys from Acklins Island who launched the old boat into calm currentless waters might have been the victims of any number of nautical mishaps that combined with poor communications between the islands led them to their fate.

The fate of the two keepers of Great Isaacs Light offers many possibilities, especially to those who believe in the supernatural. Possibly one fell into the water, and the other went to his rescue, and the tidal currents swept both to sea. Or one might have gone berserk killing both the other and himself. The number of potential answers would make a chapter alone.

The mysterious phantom plane off Daytona Beach offers the greatest puzzle of nearly any happening that has occurred in the "Devil's Triangle." All the witnesses could not have been in error as to what they saw. The only fair comment would be, How does one explain the unknown?

10. The Ghostships

The rigging straining against the deadeyes creaked a doleful tempo in rhythm with the sluggish roll of the schooner as she lay dead in the long Atlantic swell. Her teak decks betrayed traces of recent holystoning. The head- and foresails were smartly furled over their booms indicating that the task had been carried out with time to spare. The big mainsail was luffing wantonly as its boom slammed recklessly from rail to rail with each heave of the vessel. It was evident that she had been hove to before the wind petered out. Every line not in use was coiled or flaked down in Bristol fashion, and no loose gear was lying about. The two dories lashed down atop the main cabin appeared to have been the only small boats ever carried aboard. The open galley door banged in cadence with the ship's movement.

Captain Baker looked back over his right shoulder to make sure the four crewmen were still behind him. Instinctively he smashed his boot down pulverizing a thumb-sized cockroach into the deck as he motioned his men forward with the Colt revolver he was

160

holding. For the umpteenth time he bellowed out, "Halloo, thar . . . anybody aboard?" The only reply was the galley door slamming shut at the same time the main boom block struck the starboard rail. As the five men reached the bow, Captain Baker leaned against the anchor capstan and ordered his men to open a cargo hatch. Glancing across a half mile of water at his own ship, the *Ellen Austin,* also becalmed—its Union Jack hanging limp from the yard-arm—and the remainder of his crew lining the rail anxiously awaiting their captain's return, the captain thought of another ship.

That ship was found adrift with her crew missing nine years earlier east of the Azores. On December 5, 1872, the brigantine *Mary Celeste* was discovered under reduced sail ghosting along on a starboard tack at slightly over one knot. Her course was most irregular. As the British barkentine *Dei Gratia* closed the distance between the two ships, her crew could see no one on the *Mary Celeste*'s deck nor were the lifeboats still aboard. The *Dei Gratia*'s first mate, Oliver Deveau, and two seamen, John Johnson and John Wright, boarded the vessel and found not a soul aboard. There was some weather damage and several feet of water in the bilges but far from enough to endanger the vessel. A prize crew from the *Dei Gratia* was placed aboard the derelict, and the two vessels arrived without incident in Gibraltar on December 13. No trace of the *Mary Celeste*'s crew was ever found.

But Captain Baker was not aboard a weather-beaten derelict. The schooner was most seaworthy and in a well-maintained condition. The two sailing vessels had been becalmed within sight of each other for several days before they drifted to within hailing distance on August 20, 1881. Receiving no reply to his signals, the captain and four men rowed over in a dory to investigate the strange craft. She will make a fine prize, thought the captain.

"She's full of lumber," echoed a voice from the hold. "Looks like mahogany." The ship was apparently en route from Honduras or some other Central American lumber-producing area. Having been found halfway between the Bahamas and Bermuda, she was probably bound for England or the Mediterranean. Her log was missing as were the trail boards with her name. Nothing could be found to identify the vessel or anyone who had been aboard her. There was no indication, whatsoever, of any violence. And unlike the *Mary Celeste*, there was no damage to the ship. She was fully stocked with provisions and supplies.

Upon his return to the *Ellen Austin*, Captain Baker organized a prize crew, which he placed aboard his "new" ship. The orders were that as soon as the wind picked up, the two vessels would head for Boston, the *Ellen Austin*'s original destination before she had to work her way southward because of head winds.

For two days the vessels drifted within sight of each other. At times they were even within earshot of one another. By the end of the second day, the long, slow-moving swells had receded, transforming the windless sea into a flat glaring calm. The captain ordered both schooners to batten down everything and prepare to heave to. His sailor's instinct forewarned him that the abnormally still air was an omen that a drastic weather change would soon bear down on the two sailing craft even though the barometers on both vessels indicated no change.

When the change hit shortly before midnight, it brought a full gale out of the northeast. So sudden was the transition from tranquility to turmoil that the ships barely had time to hoist their storm sails and heave to. The experienced seamen aboard the two ships knew that somewhere to the southwest there blew a severe storm. They were right in their knowledge, for several hundred miles to the southwest a hurricane was blasting its way along the eastern Bahamas and eventually smashed through Georgia, Alabama, and Mississippi. Over seven hundred lives were lost in that howling fury.

The lookouts aboard the *Ellen Austin* were able to observe their prize's navigation lights throughout the night. Just as the first gray streaks of dawn began to appear in the east, rain squalls moved in. The intensity of the wind was such that the rain was driven horizontally across the surface of the sea. Facing in any direction except downwind made it impossible for anyone to open his eyes—let alone observe the prize ship.

After two days the gale worked its way around to the southeast and that brought ideal sailing weather. The sun burned through the overcast as all sails aboard the *Ellen Austin* were set. But she was alone on an empty sea. One man climbed the sail hoops to the gaff of the mainmast from where he scanned from horizon to horizon for the missing prize. Captain Baker kept one eye glued to his telescope. Every hand who wasn't engaged in working the ship was watching for the other vessel. For two days the *Ellen Austin's* crew saw only an empty expanse of ocean.

As dawn broke on the third day, the lookout called down to the deck that there was a sail barely visible on the horizon two points off the port bow. The captain, summoned from his breakfast, rushed out onto the deck with telescope in hand. He could make out the sails through his glass, but the vessel's hull was still below the horizon. He was able to perceive, however, that it was a schooner rig. As the ship's course was being changed toward the schooner, Captain Baker clambered up into the rigging with his telescope. Standing on a ratline with one arm wrapped around a mainmast shroud he brought the glass to his eye. It was the missing schooner.

As the *Ellen Austin* converged on its prize, everyone aboard from captain to cabin boy was aware that something was amiss aboard it. She was sailing in a capricious manner. So erratic was her course that Captain Baker's whaleboat had to pursue her for nearly an hour before they were finally able to board her.

With the whaleboat warped astern, the men immediately spread out and searched the ship from stem to stern. Not a trace of their shipmates could they find. Not only was the prize crew missing, but there was not even a clue that they had ever been aboard —food and provisions were untouched, bunks were never slept in, and the new logbook was nowhere to be found. The navigation lights had burned dry. They had been filled with whale oil right after the prize crew took over and could burn continuously for three days. It was as though no one had ever been placed aboard her in the first place.

Captain Baker was not only a skeptical individual, but he was also a very determined man. And he meant to get both ships back to port. After what must have been a considerable amount of persuasion by the captain, another prize crew was placed aboard the mysterious craft. Their orders were to constantly remain within sight of the *Ellen Austin*. A lifeboat fully provisioned was towed astern. The "persuaded" men were directed to abandon ship at the first sign of anything unusual. All were armed. Three shots were to be fired as an emergency signal. Except when actually working the ship, the men were to remain in sight of each other at all times. In addition to the regular half hour ringing of the ship's bell an extra ring was to be sounded on the quarter hour.

Everything went along fine until the afternoon of the second day when the sky became overcast and a light drizzling rain set in. Visibility was reduced to half a mile. The wind diminished to less than five knots. The two schooners were ghosting along at no more than two knots. Then the prize ship seemed to be dropping behind. Before those on the *Ellen Austin* realized what was happening and could bring their craft about, the prize was slowly engulfed in the watery haze. No more than ten ship lengths had separated the two vessels.

Within fifteen minutes the *Ellen Austin* was back to the spot where the prize was last seen, but the crew saw only rain and sea. Silence was maintained as all hands listened for sounds of the other vessel. But they heard only their ship's wash and the sound of the raindrops pattering the deck. There was no signal heard. Guns were fired into the air, the foghorn was blown, voices yelled, and the ship's bell clanged away periodically. Still, there was no reply. The "ghostship" had vanished and so had one-third of the *Ellen Austin*'s crew. None were ever seen or heard from again.

Another famous ghostship was the five-masted schooner *Carroll A. Deering*, owned by the C. G. Deering Co. of Portland, Maine, with Captain Willis B. Wormwell commanding. So baffling was the mystery of this ship that five different governmental departments in Washington investigated the case including the State Department, the Treasury Department, the Navy Department, the Department of Commerce, and the Department of Justice. Their combined consensus was that the *Carroll A. Deering* had been a victim of twentieth-century pirates, possibly operating from a Russian ship.

The schooner had departed Norfolk in September, 1920, bound for Rio de Janiero with a cargo of general merchandise and coal. Upon arrival in Brazil, the *Deering* was immediately off-loaded. She was then reloaded with another cargo that was destined for Norfolk. The schooner left Rio de Janiero on December 2 for Barbados.

When the *Deering*, during the first week of January, 1921, lay at anchor off Bridgetown, rumors circulated about Captain Wormwell's having had problems with some members of his crew en route to the island. That was a familiar story as three years earlier another ship had arrived at this same island from Rio de Janiero with similar rumors of its crew having engaged in disturbances en route. The other vessel's voyage had originated in Norfolk; she had sailed to Brazil, departed that port for Barbados, and then set off for Norfolk. But she never reached Norfolk. She was, of course, the *Cyclops*.

Before the *Deering* sailed from Barbados, Captain Wormwell had to bail his mate, Charles McLellan, out of jail for drunk and disorderly conduct. With half her crew drunk, the schooner departed for Norfolk on January 9, still following the track of the *Cyclops*.

On the afternoon of January 23, 1921, she sailed past the lightship *Cape Fear* off the North Carolina coast. The men aboard the lightship noticed nothing unusual as the big schooner passed. Four days later hurricane-force winds ripped down on the North Carolina coast. By January 29, the winds had diminished somewhat, but conditions were still not ideal. On that Saturday afternoon, the *Deering* approached the lightship *Cape Lookout* off Diamond Shoals about ninety miles from

Cape Fear. She was moving at a speed of five knots as she closed the distance to the lightship. When the two vessels were within hailing distance, a man aboard the schooner with red hair, who was definitely not Captain Wormwell, yelled across to the captain of the lightship, Thomas Jacobson, "We lost both anchors while riding out the storm. Can you report it ashore for us?"

Captain Jacobson later testified that the man did not give the impression of being a ship's officer and spoke with a foreign accent. The lightship captain was unable to send the message as his wireless was not working. Aside from her missing anchors, the *Deering* appeared to be in good condition.

A short time after the schooner passed the lightship, an unidentifiable steamer sailed by. The lightship signaled her to take a message, but the signal was ignored. Numerous attempts were made by the lightship's master to communicate with the passing ship, but no response was received. She continued to steam on in the same direction as the *Deering* had. In desperation, Captain Jacobson blasted away four times on the whistle, an international emergency signal. Still he was ignored.

As day broke on January 31, the men who manned the Diamond Shoals lifesaving station discovered the five-master hard up on the shoals along the outer banks. All sails were set except the two outer jibs. Waves were breaking over the length of the schooner. The men from the lifesaving station attempted to reach the grounded vessel in their surfboat, but high seas prevented their boarding her. They could see that the vessel was abandoned and that the lifeboats were gone. For four days the breaking seas lashed the vessel as howling winds ripped her, beating sails into ribbons.

When the seas finally abated to a point where the *Deering* could be boarded, members of the lifesaving station crew and coast guard officials inspected her. Aside from two cats that had managed to survive the punishing seas that had swept over the vessel, she was completely abandoned. Apparently the crew had vacated the ship in somewhat of a hurry. There was evidence that a meal was being prepared at the time the incident occurred. Most of the provisions, clothing, and supplies had been removed. The *Deering*'s rudder and steering mechanism were damaged during the grounding. The binnacle and compass had been smashed, drawers and cabinets were open, and a general disorderliness prevailed throughout the schooner. The motor lifeboat and dory were missing. Most of the charts, the log, and the navigation instruments were gone. The crew was never seen again, and the two boats or their wreckage were not found.

A number of days were to pass before the press jumped on the story. A front page *New York Times* story datelined Washington, June 20, stated, "The crew of an American ship is missing, and what seems to be conclusive evidence has been obtained that the men were taken as prisoners to another vessel and carried away to parts unknown, if they were not murdered."

Captain O. W. Parker of the Marine Shipping Board stated, "Piracy without a doubt still exists as it has since the days of the Phoenicians." Shipowners were divided in their opinions. Some thought it unlikely that pirates and sea robbers could prey on ships in the twentieth century when wireless apparatus aboard vessels was becoming almost universal, commerce lanes on the oceans more crowded than ever before, and international patrols keeping close watch on what was going on. Other shippers attributed unexplained shipping losses to World War I mines that eventually separated from their moorings and floated about the seas. Shipping owners familiar with tramp steamers and sailing vessels believed that piracy had again reared its ugly head.

On June 22, the *Times* carried the following headline: "More Ships Added to Mystery List." Between October, 1920, and February, 1921, at least ten ships vanished in the western Atlantic. They received little play in the press until the *Carroll A. Deering* incident became a front-page story. These vessels are listed in the Voyages to Nowhere chapter of this book.

The one item that fueled the theory of piracy and kidnapping on the high seas more than any other was a bottle with a note in it that was found on the beach at Buxton, North Carolina, on April 11 by Christopher Columbus Gray. The message in the bottle read, "*Deering* captured by oil-burning boat something like chaser, taking off everything, handcuffing crew. Crew hiding all over ship. No chance to make escape. Finder please notify headquarters of Deering." Many scoffed at the message as a hoax. But was it a hoax?

Facing skepticism and ridicule, Mrs. W. B. Wormwell, wife of the schooner's captain, followed up one clue after another with a Sherlock Holmes-like skill. She approached the families of each of the missing crew members and obtained a handwriting sample of every man who had crewed on the *Deering*. The vessel's owners provided her with signatures obtained when the men signed on aboard the ship. She obtained the note that was in the bottle from the customs house in Norfolk. Armed with the message and the handwriting samples, she had three different handwriting experts analyze the writings. They confirmed her previous suspicions that the note was written by

Henry Bates of Islesboro, Maine, the schooner's engineer (as engineer on a sailing vessel, he would have maintained the lifeboat motor and the deck machinery). Mrs. Wormwell also learned from experts in Washington, who had examined both the paper the message was written on and the bottle, that the paper was made in Norway and imported to Brazil in large quantities. She was also informed that the bottle was manufactured in Buenos Aires. These facts combined with the lightship's report of the strange steamer following the *Deering* pointed to piracy. Had UFO believers been as prevalent then as they are today, no doubt there would have been additional explanations put forth concerning the crew that disappeared.

Although it was proved that the bottle and its message were authentic, nothing has ever been published by either the press or government about the fate of the missing crew. It is possible that the men of the *Carroll A. Deering* were kidnapped and more than likely slain by their abductors. During Prohibition, many individuals reaped great profits. Barbados, like most other West Indian islands, was a stepping-off place for U.S.-bound rum-running vessels. A vessel the size of the *Deering* could easily transport enough liquor to be worth over a million dollars ashore in the United States.

Just outside the twelve-mile limit of the eastern seaboard, there was an area known as "Rum Row." It was here that the contraband cargoes were transferred to smaller vessels for the dash into shore. Many foreigners were engaged in this trade including a number of "big-fisted, rough-and-tumble" Finns. Because the hoodlum element would go through anything, including murder, to get their illegal cargoes ashore, they were referred to as the "go through guys." There are cases on record where "go through guys" murdered the crews of the larger ships bringing the liquor to "Rum Row" if they thought the cargo was worth the risk. Sometimes inexperienced rumrunners were hijacked, and if the crews resisted, they were murdered. It is not beyond the realm of possibility that the crew of the *Carroll A. Deering*, enticed by the thought of big profits, took on a load of liquor at Barbados or even South America and had a confrontation with the "go through guys" as they approached "Rum Row." Some people in the trade had obtained war surplus subchasers such as mentioned in the bottle message.

A later check revealed that among the crew of the *Deering* there was no one who spoke with a foreign accent and had red hair like the man who spoke to the lightship. Could the men on the schooner's deck seen by the lightship crew have been hijackers waiting to be taken off by their own ship—the strange steamer that appeared shortly afterward?

The Bahama Islands are considered to have the finest and safest waters of all the oceans. Thousands and thousands of yachts and other small vessels cruise these waters each year. One is seldom more than a day from land and in most cases but a few hours. Except during inclement weather the waters are crystal clear. Many movies supposedly filmed underwater in other parts of the world are actually filmed here. Not only are the islands a mecca for yachtsmen, but a million tourists arriving by cruise ship and airplane visit the islands annually. The group consists of 690 islands and 2,387 uninhabited rocky cays. Starting from Bimini, forty-five miles east of Miami, they extend for over six hundred miles to the east and the same distance north to south from Walker Cay to Great Inagua. They are peaceful. They are near tropical. And they are tranquilizing.

But things do happen in the Bahama Islands. Boats get wrecked on reefs. Others get lost and have to be rescued by the coast guard or the Bahama Air Sea Rescue Service. Airplanes attempting to fly through squalls are forced down at sea. On occasion hurricanes strike the area wiping out whole harbors—boats, docks, and all. And from time to time an airplane, a yacht, or a ship will simply disappear. All over the Bahamas there are shells of little pink or white houses whose owners never came home, for all of the Bahama Islands are in the "Devil's Triangle."

The economic hub and political center of the islands is Nassau, which lies just south of and approximately 150 miles east of Miami. Five hundred miles to the southeast of Nassau are the Turks Islands. Although not politically part of the Bahamas, they are geographically the easternmost of the group. Politically the people are Jamaican, and the islands are a dependency of the Jamaican government. The Turks Islands, Grand Turk and Little Turk, are bleak and barren. Until the 1960s their eight hundred souls derived their meager incomes from harvesting salt from the numerous salt ponds abounding in the island, fishing, and raising cattle, sheep and pigs. The biggest event in the lives of the Turks Islanders was being able to save enough money to make a pilgrimage to Nassau about once every five years. There is no harbor as such. Larger vessels calling there anchor off the settlement of Cockburn Town. Transportation between ships and the island is via small boats.

On December 2, 1946, the two-masted schooner *City Belle* en route from the Dominican Republic to Nassau with a cargo of lumber paid a call at Cockburn Town. The anchor had no sooner been dropped than the ship was surrounded by a fleet of small boats that had come out to unload several thousand board feet of lumber. The work progressed with great haste, for the halo around the afternoon sun meant but one thing to the native crews—a weather change for the worse. The waters surrounding the Turks Islands were not the best place for a 120-foot-long deep-draft schooner to be caught in during dirty weather. After expeditiously off-loading the consignment destined for the island, the last boat, loaded to the gunwales, headed for shore. By now the prevailing southeast wind had veered to the south. By night or early morning it would work around to the west, and then to the north bringing with it a cold front.

Four of the schooner's ten-man native crew were already leaning on their capstan bars ready to hoist the vessel's anchor. Several hands were busily passing mail sacks, brought out by one of the boats, down into the forward hold.

Beating its way out to the *City Belle* from the only dock at Cockburn Town was a native fishing smack no longer than twenty to twenty-two feet from stem to stern with a beam one-third that size. Her sails resembled a seagoing quilt work as patches had replaced nearly all of the original canvas. In addition to its two-man crew there were twenty-two passengers—men, women, and children—aboard the small craft. They were sitting along both gunwales, on the bow sprit, in the bottom, and atop each other. An occasional wave would splash over the rail. When too much water had accumulated in the boat, several of the passengers would swing their legs over the side enabling others to bail out the water with old rusted paint cans. Then the dangling legs would be swung back inboard. This procedure occurred at least every five minutes during the boat's thirty-minute trip out to the schooner. Their luggage, consisting of a few vintage suitcases such as salesmen use for samples plus several dozen straw bags jam-packed full of clothes, food, live chickens, and other items that defied description, lay in the sloshing bilge waters. All were looking forward to spending Christmas week in Nassau.

As the little boat with its human cargo banged against the nineteen-inch tires suspended over the schooner's side, her patchwork sail was dropped. Twenty-two blacks scampered and helped each other over the ship's bulwark. Crying babies and wet cackling chickens were passed from arms to arms. Suitcases and straw bags, getting lighter by the second as the water drained from them, were last to be taken aboard. As the "commuter" boat cast off for shore, the capstan crew began hoisting the anchor. As the fore- and headsails were raised, the mainsail, which had been holding the bow into the wind, was slackened off, and the big schooner was under way.

The next day the winds would be out of the north, and the *City Belle* would be close-hauled beating northwest across the Crooked Island Passage toward the Exuma Islands. And that is when it happened.

On December 5, 1946, seventy-four years to the day after the deserted derelict *Mary Celeste* was discovered with all hands missing, and exactly one year after the disappearance of Flight 19, the schooner *City Belle* was found adrift and completely deserted about three hundred miles southeast of Miami. A crash boat from a United States Naval Base on Great Exuma Island had discovered the forsaken vessel while on a routine patrol. It had been three days since the schooner departed Turks Islands. Reports on the vessel's condition indicated that there had not been any violence aboard. And like the prize vessel that the *Ellen Austin* had discovered, her cargo of lumber was intact, and the ship was in a seaworthy condition. The records and mail were removed and delivered to the British commissioner at Great Exuma. The ship's log gave no indication as to why the vessel was abandoned. Everything had been shipshape aboard her. Even the passengers' personal effects remained aboard. Only the lifeboats were missing.

An immediate sea and air search for the missing voyagers was commenced. Every island, even those remotely near the *City Belle*'s route, was checked. Natives passed word from island to island, but no trace of either survivors or lifeboats was ever found. Speculation in Nassau shipping circles centered on the likelihood that the crew and passengers had abandoned ship during high winds accompanying a cold front that churned those waters for three days. Yet the *City Belle*, when found, was not in any danger of foundering. Had she been discovered by a private, rather than a government, vessel and salvage claims initiated leading to a court hearing, there is little doubt that the mystery of the *City Belle* would rival that of the *Mary Celeste* in notoriety. But nevertheless, thirty-two more names were added to the chronicle of the "Devil's Triangle."

In 1968, the *Times* of London sponsored a single-handed, nonstop, around-the-world sailing yacht race. Ten men with their hopes set on winning the $13,500 prize sailed from England at various times. On Thursday, October 31, 1968, Donald Crowhurst, the last of the ten contestants, cast off from Teignmouth, England, aboard his forty-one-foot trimaran *Teignmouth Electron*. All ten entrants had departed at various times. The prize was not for the first to finish, but rather to the boat making the circumnavigation in the shortest length of time.

On April 22, 1969, after 312 days at sea, Englishman Robin Knox-Johnston sailed his thirty-two-foot ketch, *Suhaili*, into Falmouth—the first and only finisher as of that date. French contestant Bernard Motessier might have won, but decided to put in to Tahiti rather than return to the pitfalls of civilization. Others were forced out due to sickness or damage to their crafts. Only Crowhurst remained at sea and was still in the running.

On June 23, Crowhurst, an electronics engineer, sent a radio message to his wife that he was becalmed with less than two thousand miles to go. He reported his position as being about seven hundred miles southwest of the Azores. He had been at sea for 248 days and would finish the race within two weeks. It appeared that Donald Crowhurst was to be the winner. Celebrations, wild welcomings, press conferences, product endorsements, television offers, and his wife and four children awaited the thirty-six-year-old yachtsman's victorious homecoming.

Shortly before 8 A.M. on July 10, 1969, at latitude 33 degrees and 11 minutes north and 40 degrees and 28 minutes west, which is about seven hundred miles west of the Azores, the royal mail vessel *Picardy*, Captain Richard Box commanding, came across a ketch-rigged trimaran ghosting along under mizzen sail only. A close inspection revealed no one on deck. In order to assure that everything was all right aboard the trimaran so far at sea, the *Picardy's* whistle was sounded. But still no one appeared on deck. The captain sent a lifeboat with four men to investigate. The boat turned out to be the *Teignmouth Electron*, but Donald Crowhurst was nowhere to be found. The dinghy and life raft were secured in place, and except for the general untidiness common to small boats being sailed by lone sailors over vast empty waters, everything was shipshape. Here on the outer fringes of the "Devil's Triangle" a boat whose voyage was being followed by all of England had been discovered in a most baffling plight. Could round-the-world sailor Donald Crowhurst have fallen overboard on the final leg of his race home? A possibility, but not very likely for a sailor who had been at sea continuously for over 252 days. Then what? UFOs? A space or time warp creating a change of dimension? A sea monster? Atlanteans? Scores of theories were brought forth. Hugo Vihlen, who on June 21, 1968, completed an eighty-five-day transatlantic voyage alone in the *April Fool,* a bathtub-sized sailboat less than six feet long, suggested that a fate befell Crowhurst that nearly happened to him as he was crossing the "Devil's Triangle."

Vihlen, whose record for having sailed the Atlantic in the smallest boat ever, still stands, stated, "I took the morning off on May 19, which I really needed to do. I almost took forever off. I went swimming, easing myself into the water, and was completely in before I realized I didn't have my safety line on. The boat was rigged for self-steering, and would have left me a nice thousand-mile swim. I clambered back aboard in a real big hurry."* Could Crowhurst have taken a swim without using a safety line, and when a gust of wind came up, been unable to swim fast enough to reach the *Teignmouth Electron*? Sir Francis Chichester referred to the mystery as the "sea drama of the century."

*Hugo S. Vihlen, *April Fool* (Chicago: Follett Publishing Co., 1971).

Within a twelve-day period of the strange discovery of the *Teignmouth Electron,* no less than four other deserted yachts were found drifting in the same general section of the Atlantic Ocean. One of these was the twenty-foot sloop *Vagabond* being sailed alone from Stockholm, Sweden, to Australia by Peter Wallin. The Swedish motor ship *Golar Frost,* en route from Puerto Cortés, Honduras, to Genoa, Italy, discovered the *Vagabond* under full sail, flying the Swedish flag, but with Wallin missing. Everything aboard the sloop was in good condition. On July 4, the British steamer *Cotopaxi* reported finding a yacht heading east with the automatic steering set, but not a soul aboard. Another British ship, the tanker *Helisoma,* discovered a sixty-nine-footer floating bottom up. Off the coast of northwest Africa a British motor ship, *The Maplebank,* reported sighting a sixty-foot-long vessel floating keel up. "It's rare to get reports like this in such a close area in such a vast ocean," said a spokesman of Lloyd's Shipping Exchange. He added, "It is rather odd."

Something had happened to Donald Crowhurst, and that made excellent newspaper copy for several weeks. Then the "sea drama of the century" was solved. The *Picardy* had hoisted Crowhurst's boat aboard, and after searching the area for any sign of the trimaran's skipper, proceeded on to Santo Domingo, her destination. A logbook containing a number of strange entries, a tape recorder, and a movie camera were among the things found aboard the racing trimaran. After studying these items, Captain Box and officials discovered that Crowhurst had not been on the last leg of an around the world race. Instead he had spent the previous six months cruising in the South Atlantic and entering false reports in his logbooks. It was further discovered (his tapes and logbook entries verified this) that the thought of a fraudulent victory had played upon Donald Crowhurst's mind to such an extent that on July 1 he lowered himself over the side and let the *Teignmouth Electron* sail off without him. An incredible explanation, but true.

What if Donald Crowhurst had taken his tape recorder and logbook with him when he decided to end it all? His disappearance would be labeled as another great unsolved mystery of the sea. If the facts concerning other "ghostships" were discovered, would they too prove to be the results of earthbound causes? There are numerous cases on record of deranged seamen going berserk and killing all hands before committing suicide. Now if one were to throw all of his victims overboard before jumping over the side himself, and this may well have happened on occasion, the legend of another ghostship would be born.

Every book or article written on the "Devil's Triangle" has included the story of the Cuban freighter *Rubicon*, which was sighted by a navy blimp drifting off Florida's east coast on October 21, 1944. A coast guard cutter from Miami was dispatched to the scene. Daring very high seas the coast guardsmen boarded the *Rubicon*. A dog was the only living thing aboard the ship. The vessel was in a seaworthy condition with everything aboard intact. However, a lifeboat was missing, and a broken hawser was hanging over the bow. That is all that is ever mentioned about the "ghostship" *Rubicon*.

But was the *Rubicon* a "ghostship" that merits the notoriety given it down through the years? It is true that the vessel was found with its crew missing and only a dog aboard, but that is only part of the story—the part that makes good reading. According to the National Oceanic and Atmospheric Administration, from October 12 to October 20, 1944, a killer hurricane with winds up to 158 miles per hour ripped across the western part of Cuba, roared up the Florida peninsula, and ravaged the entire eastern seaboard of the United States leaving at least fifty-four dead on its two-thousand-mile rampage. Damage in the United States alone was in excess of sixty million dollars.

The hawser hanging over the *Rubicon*'s bow probably was secured to a sea anchor during the storm and eventually parted. Unable to maintain steerage on the vessel, the crew panicked and took to the lifeboat (the one missing). The dog, perhaps terrified by the pitching and tossing of the ship, was probably cowering in a cubbyhole someplace, and the crew did not take the time to find the creature. With winds up to 158 miles per hour, the lifeboat and its occupants stood little chance of survival and perished in the tempest.

To surmise that panic has accounted for more lives lost in the "Devil's Triangle" than have occurrences bordering on the occult seems safe. Contributing equally to deaths in the "triangle" is poor judgment, and there is no doubt that one or both of these situations led to the loss of the *Rubicon*'s crew. However, the situations aboard the *City Belle* and the *Ellen Austin*'s prize ship showed no evidence of panic. As to poor judgment, we will never know.

A "ghost" vessel that has received as much, if not more, printed space as the *Rubicon* was the yacht *Connemara IV* hailing from New York. She was found crewless and adrift some four hundred miles southwest of Bermuda in September, 1955. The large yacht was somewhat battered but still afloat and sound. Here is another situation where writers have overlooked causes other than the occult. Yet what the

Connemara IV experienced was as melodramatic as any sea story ever written. Along the *Connemara IV*'s track from New York to where she was found there passed Hurricane "Connie" during the second week in August with winds up to one hundred miles per hour. Less than a week later Hurricane "Diane" with its 125 miles per hour winds roared over the exact same area and claimed over two hundred lives. But there was more to come for the yacht *Connemara IV*. Within two weeks Hurricane "Ione" battered the identical sector of the "Devil's Triangle" with its 125 miles per hour winds.

Most blue-water sailors agree that for the crew of a yacht to have remained at sea continuously for a month and to be belted by three hurricanes during that period would be almost beyond human endurance.

The only mystery about the yacht *Connemara IV* is, How did she manage to survive three consecutive hurricanes? One can only comprehend the ferocity of a hurricane at sea by living through the experience. But to survive one storm and to have another strike even before the waves and seas of the first have diminished and then to have yet a third slam in is almost unthinkable.

11. Recent Developments

When I started writing this book in the summer of 1973, the eleven individuals involved in the two most recent occurrences in the "Devil's Triangle" were alive and well. Most of them listened to Vincent Price tell of ships that voyaged into the unknown, planes that climbed skyward never to return, and yachts that simply vanished as they watched the TV film *The Devil's Triangle*.* They had no apprehension as they watched that they, also, would one day experience the curse of these fatal waters.

At first light on December 20, 1973, the fifty-one-foot Chris Craft Constellation *Sea Boy II* cleared the buoy at Bell Channel leading out of the yacht basin at Freeport in the Bahama Islands. The white-hulled cabin cruiser was bound for Nassau 120 miles to the southeast. Twenty-eight-year-old Michael Baldwin, the yacht's operator, looked back at the diverging wake as he set the throttles at cruising speed. The night lights in the large resort city were beginning

*Verified by next of kin.

to flicker out with the onrushing dawn, but the glaring red sunlight reflected back to the southeast by the glass panes of thousands of oceanfront hotel windows gave the illusion of the rooms being lit from within by floodlights. Baldwin steadied his course on 125 degrees. Ahead the sea spread out like a huge sheet of sunlit tinfoil. A gentle prevailing wind was out of the southeast. The *Sea Boy's* bow was heading right into it.

Below in the main cabin Baldwin's cousin Billy Mazzulo, twenty-six, and his uncle Dick Mazzulo, thirty-five, sat sipping coffee as they watched Billy's twenty-two year-old wife Kathy preparing breakfast. Dick's wife Nancy, thirty, was in the fo'c'sle waking their three children, Robin ten; Anthony six; and Matthew, two. All looked forward to Christmas in Nassau.

As the sun rose higher so did the seas in front of the *Sea Boy*. The winds were up to ten knots and increasing. The two women cleaning up from breakfast spent more time steadying themselves than washing dishes. The three men grouped themselves by the wheel, one steering and two studying the course that Mazzulo had plotted. Perhaps they also discussed plans to meet Bill's aunt, Eleanor Baldwin, the boat's owner, who was to fly from Washington, D.C., to join them in Nassau for Christmas. The three children, lying on the deck in the sun, enjoyed the occasional splashes from the flying spray. Baldwin maintained a speed of twelve knots in order to conserve fuel, for he had heard in Freeport that diesel fuel was scarce and expensive in Nassau due to the energy crisis. The wind, gusting to fifteen knots, was working around to the south. Seas were four feet with an occasional wave of six feet. The two women came up topside complaining that it was too rough below. Baldwin eased off on the throttles slightly and suggested that Bill and Dick go below to close the ports and check to see that the Christmas presents stowed in the spare cabin were all right.

Soon the wind was up to a steady fifteen knots and blowing right out of the south. Seas were averaging six feet, and Baldwin slowed the engines. The *Sea Boy II* plowed along at less than ten knots. Baldwin was sweating, for he had closed the windows to keep out the salt spray. The children were pretending that their stomachs weren't feeling woozy. At times the wind seemed to be working more to the west, and the boat both pitched and rolled as the waves swept in from two different directions.

As the wind shifted to blow directly out of the west, the boat rolled more vigorously. Studying the position plot, prepared by Dick Mazzulo, who was the ship's navigator, the men decided that they were as close to the Berry Islands as they were to Freeport. And once they reached the Berrys, they could proceed along the eastern side of those islands and be protected from the rising seas now out of the west. They would be approaching the northernmost of the group in another two hours.

The *Sea Boy's* two GM 671 diesels maintained a steady rhythm as they propelled the fifteen-year-old vessel through the choppy cross seas. Dick Mazzulo took the wheel. Baldwin and Billy Mazzulo went below to prepare lunch. The two women made an effort to relax in their sliding deck chairs, while the three children, crouched on the afterdeck, watched diving sea gulls following the vessel's wake. From a jet plane flying high above, the white cabin cruiser appeared to be just another whitecap in the breaking seas.

After a time the seas driven by the west wind caused the *Sea Boy II* to roll as much as twenty degrees. How-

ever, the fore and aft pitching motion had lessened.
The helmsman brought the boat's speed back up to
around ten knots. The Berry Islands would appear on
the horizon in less than an hour. The wind was approaching twenty knots. Small-craft warnings were
raised throughout Florida and the Bahamas.

The hour passed and all eyes aboard the *Sea Boy II*
strained ahead; then slowly, ever so slowly, lifting
above the horizon was the light tower on Great Stirrup Cay, the northernmost island of the Berry group.
The women must have had a feeling of relief. It
wouldn't be long before the yacht would be protected
from the seas rolling in out of the west by the chain
of islands running almost northwest to southeast for
over twenty-five miles along their course.

To be on a vessel that has been storm tossed continuously for hours and suddenly enter a quiet body
of water behind a coral reef or island is a feeling com-
parable to getting off some wild amusement park
ride that is about to make you sick to your stomach.
And that is how some of those aboard the *Sea Boy II*
must have felt when the vessel reached the lee side
of Great Stirrup Cay. With the smoother water, they
could now run the boat at a normal speed for at least
two hours before being exposed to seas out of the
west again Then it would be only an hour and a half
to Nassau. The Berry Islands are located on the
northeastern tip of the Great Bahama Bank—a huge
shoal looming out of the depths upon which sits more
than half the Bahama Islands. The Berrys are a low-
lying group with maximum elevation on any of the
islands being no more than fifty feet. Along the western side of the islands are vast areas of shallows with
occasional anchorages and small harbors. The east
side consists mostly of coquina ledges under which
the water deepens rather rapidly and is exposed to the

prevailing easterlies. Most of the Berrys are inhabited. Several are privately owned. The east shore offers little protection from storms out of any easterly direction. There are several channels connecting the east and west sides, but a considerable amount of local knowledge is needed to get through them unscathed in rough weather. These islands do form a breakwater against storms coming out of the west. And that is what those aboard the *Sea Boy* found.

Once sheltered the *Sea Boy II* was run flat out at eighteen knots in order to make up for time lost bucking head seas all morning. Those aboard hoped to make Nassau by dark. The waters along the eastern shore of the Berrys drop right off. The yacht moved along less than a hundred yards from shore, yet the water was over forty feet deep. The winds seemed to be intensifying, but the waters passing under the boat's hull were almost glass smooth.

Nearing the southern end of the Berry chain, the *Sea Boy II* was forced to slow down. A heavy surge from the west was sweeping around Whale Cay. The farther south the yacht sailed the rougher it became. The wind, varying between west and northwest, was in excess of twenty-five knots. The seas were running eight to ten feet. The three men, apparently deciding that to go on would endanger not only the vessel but the lives of those aboard, brought the *Sea Boy II* about and headed back for the lee protection of the islands where they would anchor and wait for the seas to subside.

As the *Sea Boy's* anchor dug into the bottom, her bow swung around into the intensifying offshore wind. She was anchored in forty feet of water less than two hundred feet off Market Fish Cay. The island made a fine breakwater. The wind howled and roared, but the water so close to shore was as smooth as the proverbial mill pond. With the main engines secured and the auxiliary generator running, the ten-foot dinghy was placed in the water and tied astern. Being experienced skin divers and having a quantity of diving gear aboard, the three men more than likely did what every yachtsman does who cruises through the fish-abounding waters of the Berrys—they went fishing. There's nothing like a dinner of fresh-caught fish or lobster in the snug cabin of a securely anchored boat while a storm rages outside.

Meanwhile, in Washington, D.C., Eleanor Baldwin, the *Sea Boy*'s owner, left early from the trucking company where she was an executive. She had to go home and pack for her trip to Nassau the next day where she would join the party on the *Sea Boy II* for Christmas. With each ring of her telephone she expected word that the yacht had reached Nassau.

But the *Sea Boy II* was caught. What had only a short while earlier been a sheltered snug anchorage protected by an island had become a tempestuous lee shore. The wind was now out of the north. The cabin cruiser with its eight occupants was hemmed in by a raging sea on one side and a jagged coral ledge waiting like the teeth-filled jaws of a shark two hundred feet shoreward—a classic example of being caught between the "devil and the deep blue sea." Each time her bow would plunge down into an oncoming sea, the anchor line and chain would sag like a dead snake. But when the next wave lifted the bow skyward, the "dead serpent" would snap back to life as the anchor line became taut as a fiddle string about to break.

In Washington Eleanor Baldwin, not having heard from the *Sea Boy II* by the time she had finished dinner, became concerned. She calmed herself by remembering that her brother and nephews had mentioned they might stop en route to do some scuba diving and might not arrive in Nassau until late.

Before she boarded her flight the next day, she telephoned friends in Nassau to check on the *Sea Boy II*. The vessel had not yet arrived. She then called the Bahama Air-Sea Rescue Association office in Freeport. BASRA checked and told her that her boat had departed there the previous morning. BASRA in Nassau was alerted. An attempt to contact the Bahama Air-Sea Rescue Auxiliary at Chub Cay in the Berrys proved fruitless, for that radio had been out of commission for nearly twenty hours. BASRA searchers preparing to search for a lost plane were informed that they were also looking for a white fifty-one-foot yacht.

What about that missing plane? On the same morning the *Sea Boy* sailed from Freeport, the second sequence in the double tragedy began to unfold.

In Nassau, forty-six-year-old Benjamin Teetor, of Fort Lauderdale, and twenty-nine-year-old Robbie Gossman, a former Peace Corps worker from Louisville, were seated in the coffee shop of the Olympia Hotel waiting to order breakfast. They were joined by Jeff Cooper for whom they had come to Nassau to testify in a civil lawsuit. They had arrived two days previously in Teetor's personal plane. At the last minute, the magistrate postponed the hearing for several weeks, meaning Teetor and Miss Gossman had made a fruitless trip. The three had partied the night before aboard the motorsailer *Traveller III* at Yacht Haven Marina and they planned to do some shopping after which Cooper would drive Teetor and Miss Gossman to the airport.

Breakfast completed, the three strolled along Bay Street, Nassau's main thoroughfare. Normally, Christmas is a busy time in Nassau. But this year tourists were few, probably due to the fuel crisis. The warmth of the sun felt relaxing on their faces. Standing near the bronze cannons in front of Nassau's straw market, Teetor and Miss Gossman discussed their time of departure and some minor repairs the plane needed with Cooper. Teetor heard a woman's voice calling out his name. It was thirty-one-year-old Joy Loomis, also from Fort Lauderdale, and a friend of a friend. Miss Loomis mentioned that she was flying back to Florida that afternoon, and Teetor invited her to accompany them as his plane was a four seater. Miss Loomis accepted and mentioned that she might as well get a refund on her ticket. Cooper said he'd drive them to the airport whenever they were ready.

Nassau's main road to the airport leads through the town's slum area. It is mostly two lanes and little improved for as long as anyone can remember. The four crowded into Cooper's Triumph sedan with their luggage and the items they had bought in Nassau. It was nearly noon. Most of the oncoming traffic consisted of taxis bringing in tourists who had arrived on the morning planes from Florida. As the little English car topped the crest of a hill at the outskirts of Nassau, it was buffeted by a gust of wind.

At Nassau's Windsor Field Cooper dropped Teetor off at a hangar where he could obtain parts and service for his single-engine Lake amphibian plane. The women were driven out to the plane with the luggage and packages. Cooper waited by the plane until Teetor arrived with a mechanic to repair a defective brake. The repair job would take two hours. Cooper, having a business appointment in Nassau, had to leave. He exchanged farewells with the three Americans, climbed into his Triumph and drove off. He took a last look at the white-and-blue aircraft as he turned off the field.

Teetor was squatting with the mechanic next to the wheel with the defective brake, and the two women were walking toward the hangar. The red wind sock atop the control tower resembled a huge rigid finger pointing to the east.

Two hours later when the repair was completed, the wind sock was still being filled from the west. The speed of the anemometer next to it gave the illusion that the rotor was missing. Teetor walked over to the hangar to call in his flight plan. His plan was to put down at Bimini rather than cross the Gulf Stream if the weather got much worse. He checked the plane over. Even with twenty-five-knot head winds, there was more than ample fuel for the trip. If necessary, he could take on more at Bimini. The sky was clear.

The plane was cleared for takeoff by Nassau tower. Shortly before 2 P.M. Teetor raced his aircraft down the runway. Within six hundred feet it was airborne and climbing skyward. Soon the aircraft was clearing New Providence Island. Below, the yellow brown stretch of coral infested waters reached out to the west.

The demarcation line separating the midnight blue depths from the yellow brown shallow areas off the western end of New Providence is normally very pronounced from the air. As it passed under Teetor's plane, the line was almost totally obscured by the churning seas. The aircraft headed directly into the wind, which had shifted to slightly north of west.

Looking back, Teetor could see New Providence Island disappearing in the salt haze. To the southwest he could see the northern tip of Andros, the largest of all the Bahamas. Ahead and slightly to the north lay the Berry Islands. Below churned the windswept waters of the Northwest Providence Channel, one of the Bahama's inland seas. These were waters that Teetor had not only flown over on numerous occasions but had also sailed aboard the *Barracuda*, a fifty-five-foot half-sized replica of an old square-rigger that he had built in Abaco. His crew aboard the little bark usually consisted of a contingent of sea scouts and his three teen-aged sons.

In Las Olas Isles, a well-to-do section of Fort Lauderdale, the *Barracuda* was docked behind Teetor's house where it had lain idle for a number of months. The three Teetor boys, Steve, twenty, Geoffrey, sixteen; and Stuart, seventeen, were busily cleaning and making the miniature ship seaworthy for some Christmas holiday cruising. Their fourteen-year-old sister, Heidi, sat on the dock watching.

Teetor's plane was pushed at 150 knots by its two-hundred horsepower Lycoming engine, although its ground speed was less than 100 knots. Surface winds were twenty-five to thirty-five knots, but at the plane's altitude they were in excess of fifty knots. Clouds were moving in from the northwest. Teetor's plane was over the Great Bahama Bank where the average water depth is less than twelve feet. Ahead, Bimini was barely visible through the haze. Even though the plane was being buffeted about somewhat, Teetor radioed that he was canceling his scheduled stop at Bimini and would continue on to Pompano Beach's Air Park, on the mainland. He still had ample fuel, and mechanically the plane was functioning all right.

Within thirty minutes after Teetor canceled Bimini from his flight plan, cyclonic winds ripped through some areas of the western Bahamas. By this time, the plane and its three occupants would already be well out over the Florida Strait.

The Teetor boys finished working on the *Barracuda*

around four. Steve and his sister went to do some Christmas shopping. Geoffrey and Stuart stayed home to set up the Christmas tree, wrap gifts, and address cards.

Meanwhile in Nassau, Jeff Cooper received a call at 8 P.M. from Steve Teetor inquiring about his father's whereabouts. Cooper said that the plane left that afternoon. But he would call the Bahamas Air-Sea Rescue Association and have it check Bimini and other places where the plane might have landed. He instructed Steve to notify the FAA at once . . . which he did.

About this time a cold front was passing over the Bahamas and Florida. Twenty-five-knot to forty-knot winds were blowing down from the north.

On Friday morning, December 21, Jeff Cooper was notified by BASRA that Ben Teetor had not been heard of since he cancelled his scheduled stop at Bimini. The FAA had also received this word and was notifying the Coast Guard.

With the coming of daylight, the Bahamian seas had subsided, and a ten-knot wind blew from the northeast. BASRA search craft were already exploring the Berry Islands chain, and air and surface craft communicated back and forth about the *Sea Boy II* and the white-and-blue amphibian aircraft. Then two freighters, one Yugoslavian and one Liberian, both reported picking up a May Day distress signal while passing through the Northwest Providence Channel the night before. Neither was able to get a name or fix on the distressed vessel before the signal faded out. The search was intensified, then suddenly all search craft were notified the subject plane had been located.

For Steve, Stuart, Geoffrey, and Heidi Teetor it was a wonderful relief. Now their father would be home for Christmas. BASRA had notified the FAA in Miami that Ben Teetor's amphibian was parked at Bimini waiting for repairs to a damaged landing gear. All aboard were safe. Although their father hadn't contacted them yet, the children thought he would return that day, as it takes only an hour for the repair parts to reach Bimini from Miami. And if he couldn't get the parts that day, they thought he'd fly back home by commercial plane and return after Christmas to get his own plane.

But for Eleanor Baldwin, aboard an airliner bound for Nassau, there was no relief. With each mile her anxiety increased, anxiety shared by another brother, Jack Mazzulo, who was accompanying her.

The BASRA office in Nassau was monitoring the coast guard radio's working frequency 2670 on its receiver, when a search helicopter reported spotting something off Market Fish Cay that resembled a sunken boat. A boat with a diver was dispatched from Nassau.

Then a BASRA search boat radioed that it was checking out a report of wreckage washed ashore at Holmes Cay about ten miles north of where the helicoptor spotted the submerged wreckage.

As soon as they passed through customs and immigration inspection in Nassau, Eleanor Baldwin and Jack Mazzulo went directly to the BASRA office. There they awaited word from the dive boat en route to Market Fish Cay. The searchers at Holmes Cay called in that the wreckage found there could be from the missing Chris Craft. Mrs. Baldwin and her brother immediately chartered a plane and flew to Chub Cay where they hired a well-known fishing guide, Captain George, to take them to Holmes Cay in his boat.

As Captain George's boat neared Holmes Cay, those aboard overheard the dive boat radioing Nassau that

the sunken vessel was located in forty feet of water
two hundred feet east of Market Fish Cay. It went
down while at anchor and was definitely the *Sea-
Boy II*. There was no sign of either victims or survivors.

After examining the debris on Holmes Cay, consisting of a deck chair, a galley sink, a life jacket,
and a cabin side, Mrs. Baldwin and Mazzulo definitely
identified them as being from the *Sea Boy II*. Mrs.
Baldwin decided to return to Nassau and wait at the
BASRA office while the search for survivors continued.
Her brother joined the search team that was scouring
the shorelines of the various islands.

December 22 is the shortest day of the year. For
Eleanor Baldwin waiting in the BASRA office in
Nassau, it was the longest day of her life. There was
no word of hope from the various search teams.

For the Teetor children awaiting their father's
return in Fort Lauderdale, it was also a long day.
Finally, Steve called the FAA in Miami, and a message was sent to Bimini inquiring why Ben Teetor,
Robbie Gossman, and Joy Loomis hadn't left Bimini
yet. Word was sent back that the repaired Lake
amphibian had taken off the day before, except that it
was white and red—not white and blue. Thus it was
discovered that a tragic mistake had been made. The
Lake amphibian that landed in Bimini for emergency
repairs belonged to a missionary who was flying to
South America. No one in Bimini knew anything about
the white-and-blue aircraft. Its pilot and his two
women passengers had flown off into the unknown.

Eleanor Baldwin received a call from her brother
Jack who was on Bonds Cay, which is about halfway
between Holmes and Market Fish cays. The *Sea Boy's*
ten-foot dinghy had been found. But it was located a
hundred feet in from the shoreline. No one could ex-

plain how the dinghy got so far inland. No trace was
ever found of the five adults and three small children
who had been aboard the yacht.

When Jack Mazzulo met Eleanor back in Nassau,
he handed her a package still wrapped in Christmas
paper that he had found at the water's edge on
Holmes Cay. When she opened it, she saw a child's
doll. Attached to one leg of the doll was a card that
read "From Kathy—Merry Christmas."

12. Natural or Supernatural

"There is only one man aboard the *Gulf King V*, and he is losing his mind. He has been alone on his boat for five days. Would like to have an airplane try and locate the *Gulf King V*." This was part of a message received by the search and rescue section of the Seventh District Coast Guard Headquarters in Miami. The date was December 19, 1966. The message originated from the vessel *Gulf King III*, a sister ship. The two vessels were part of a fleet of shrimp boats owned by the Gulf King Ice Company of Corpus Christi, Texas.

The captain went berserk six days previously and chased the crew of five around the *Gulf King V*. Finally, the men scrambled over the side into the water to escape their menacing master. Two other Gulf King boats picked them up. The deranged captain was already heading the sixty-five-foot shrimper farther out into the Atlantic with two sister ships in pursuit.

After six days, the chase ended. Men from the other two vessels boarded the *Gulf King V*, regained control, and headed for Barbados. Thus, the incident was over for everyone except the mad captain. But there might have been a different ending. The crewmen could have fled the shrimper at night, during inclement weather, or when the rest of the Gulf King fleet was just over the horizon. In such a situation they might have perished in the sea. The captain could have kept going in the *Gulf King V*, heading farther out to sea. Eventually he would exhaust his fuel and food. It would be only a matter of time before thirst, hunger, and aimless drifting would drive him beyond all comprehension whatsoever. The wretchedness of the hot humid air in the cabin would force him out onto the deck where the parching sun's intensity would impel him back into the cabin. The ice in the hold would have melted, and the stinking odor of the rotting shrimp would only add to his plight. Whether in the shelter of the cabin or out on deck, to go on would be intolerable. He would have retrograded to a raving lunatic. There would be no reasoning left. The madman would have but one recourse—the sea. Eventually there would be a sighting of the wallowing vessel. It would be boarded. But no trace of any humans would be found, and the *Gulf King V* would be branded as a ghostship—and another legend of the "Devil's Triangle" would be born.

The purpose of telling about the *Gulf King V* is to point out how easily the ship might have become another mystery of the sea. It would have been a story that every writer of the unexplained would "explain."

Sometimes when there isn't a mystery at all, a writer will distort the facts just enough to create a mystery. Some authors will even create their own "facts." The guest on a radio talk show in Miami, during

the middle part of 1973, implied that UFOs were
the prime culprits in the "triangle." He had written
a book, *Limbo of the Lost,* in which he referred to the
area as the "Limbo." During the course of the pro-
gram, he talked about the *V. A. Fogg,* a tanker
that went down with all hands during February, 1972,
in the Gulf of Mexico. (See the chapter titled "The
Sulphur Ships.") He stated that when divers went
down to the *Fogg,* all hands were missing except the
captain whose body was found sitting in his cabin,
his hand still clutching a coffee cup. Although he did
not state it outright, he implied that UFOs were responsible for the disappearance of the missing men.
That writer's ideas are as wet as the hulk of the
V. A. Fogg, which is now resting ninety feet beneath
the Gulf of Mexico. First, a man drowning or killed
by an explosion wouldn't and couldn't hold onto a
coffee cup. Second, other bodies were found as evi-
denced by coast guard photographs. A letter to the
coast guard in Washington inquiring about the captain's coffee cup and the lack of any other crew
members' bodies was answered as follows by Captain B. L. Meaux, chief of the Public Affairs Division, "We *do not* know this to be a fact." Many
writers will twist facts somewhat for the sake of better
and more interesting reading. But to completely distort the facts is no more than sensationalism.

Another example of literary sensationalism concerns
two articles about the "triangle" that I wrote for the
August and September, 1972, issues of *Saga* magazine.
I had titled the articles "The Devil's Triangle: Part I"
and "The Devil's Triangle: Part II." There was only a
very brief reference to UFOs and no mention at all
of flying saucers. Yet when the stories came out in
print, they were titled "Bermuda Triangle—UFO Twi-

light Zone" and "The Deadly Bermuda Triangle Flying Saucer 'Space Warp' Domain." Every mention of the "Devil's Triangle" had been changed to "Bermuda Triangle." Is "Bermuda Triangle" a correct or appropriate name? If a geographical designation is to be applied to the name, it should refer to the area where the most happenings have taken place—the "Florida-Bahama Triangle."

Literary sensationalism tends to attract many hangers-on and others who want in on the action. Twenty-nine-year-old Norman Slater of Kenosha, Wisconsin, claims to have extraordinary powers of extrasensory perception. He is, or was, interested in the "Devil's Triangle." This "gifted" individual stated publicly that he had visions of three "hot spots" off the east coast of Florida within a twenty-mile radius of each other where danger awaits passing ships and other craft. Most south Florida newspapers carried Slater's press releases concerning this.

"There is a strong possibility that any ship standing on any of these spots would disappear," said Slater. He believes the victims had become trapped in a time machine situation, a sort of funnel that can hold objects in an invisible dimension for periods before suddenly releasing them again.

"Time is not a simple constant flowing quantity that we assume it to be. It may sometime release these ships and planes from the other dimension in which they are suspended, and they will return to the space from which they had vanished. I don't want to be there when it happens," says Slater. "It will be horrible, for the crews will be skeletons."

Slater was trying to obtain financing to charter a ship, crew it with dummies, and anchor it over one of the three "hot spots" that he visualized. The ships would be equipped with automatic cameras and closed circuit television. He predicted that this project would solve the mystery of the "Devil's Triangle."

Other predictions by Slater were that Nixon would defeat McGovern, but by a very narrow margin. He also foresaw marijuana being legalized in 1974. His services as an ESP consultant were engaged by a Fort Lauderdale couple whose teen-aged daughter had been missing for a number of months. He received a fee of $225. For this he informed the parents of fourteen-year-old Mary Briscolina that he would send them a letter within a few days telling them of the girl's whereabouts. Several days later, on February 3, 1973, the Briscolinas received the letter from Slater. He said their daughter was alive and well and that she would be driving by their house in a few days to see if they were all right.

Several weeks later, Briscolina released the following statement to the press: "When our daughter was already dead, already a skeleton, he [Slater] was telling us she was alive." In a suburban Fort Lauderdale field young Mary's remains had been discovered. She had been murdered and dead for over four months—since the previous October. The south Florida newspapers are no longer publishing articles about the man from Kenosha. His press agent's phone has been disconnected. Apparently Norman Slater has given up his plans to solve the mysteries of the "Devil's Triangle."

Until the sea spews forth the secrets of the "Devil's Triangle," there will always be self-proclaimed seers and sensationalists capitalizing on the sea's greatest mystery. Some will attribute the enigma to UFOs, others will blame Martians, and a few will pick up where Edgar Cayce left off and accuse Atlanteans who periodically emerge from the deepest trenches of the sea in their highly sophisticated hydrospace conveyances and abduct less intelligent, inferior earthbound human beings.

Hugo Vihlen, who sailed across the Atlantic Ocean in a little boat less than six feet long, saw nothing strange or occult during his passage through the "Devil's Triangle."

Bill Verity is known in sailing circles as a man who will go to great extremes to prove a point. In 1967, he sailed alone from Fort Lauderdale to Ireland in a twelve-foot plywood sloop. In 1969, Verity sailed from Ireland to Fort Lauderdale in a twenty-foot plywood sloop, the *St. Brenden*, in order to prove that an Irish monk, Brenden the Bold, made a similar crossing almost a thousand years before Columbus arrived in the New World. One hundred and fifteen days and 5,720 miles after departing the town of Fenit in County Kerry, Ireland, Verity arrived at San Salvador Island in the Bahamas.

While standing next to a monument commemorating Columbus's landing at that island, Verity was asked what the hardest part of his voyage had been. The barrel-chested Irishman responded, "The worst thing on the voyage was being trapped by a lightning barrage 104 days out." This experience occurred in the "triangle." The red-bearded skipper went on, "Never have I seen such lightning. Lightning bolt after lightning bolt striking the water. All hell had broken loose. I was peppered all night and the next day by huge bolts of lightning. Never seen anything like it. You could smell the ozone as they hit the water. I don't scare easily, but I was terrified that night."

This writer has voyaged through nearly every sector of the "triangle." Once when sailing from Jupiter Inlet, Florida, to West End in the Bahamas, I saw seven waterspouts at one time. Luckily we managed to avoid them. On another occasion while doing some underwater filming for General Electric on an oceanographic project fourteen miles south of Bermuda in water that was over four thousand feet deep, I saw something that had me mystified for a number of years. I had just finished filming the movement of an instrumentation buoy in rough seas. The last of my film had run through the camera when my safety diver, Pat Boatwright, grabbed me by the shoulder and pointed downward. It was late in the afternoon, and the rough seas were distorting the light rays that penetrated into the depths. What I saw was phenomenal. How deep it was or its size I couldn't tell. It might have been 100 feet beneath us—maybe 150 feet. Its size I could only guess at—maybe a hundred feet across, possibly seventy-five, but no less than fifty feet in diameter. It was perfectly round. Its color was a deep purple. It was moving slowly up toward us. At its outer perimeter there was a form of pulsation, but there was no movement of water. As we started for the surface, it stopped its ascent. Then slowly it began to descend into the blackening depths. Awestricken, we watched until it was no more.

For a number of years I was unable to determine what it was that Pat and I had seen. He theorized that it was a giant squid, but I found myself unable to agree with him. Most of the people that we mentioned it to said that we'd been underwater too long that day. In fact, they almost had me convinced that they were right. Then one day while shooting the breeze with some natives on the pier at Majuro in the Marshall Islands, half a world away from Bermuda, I found what I think is the answer to what Pat and I had seen. All around the dock from a depth of two feet up to the surface the lagoon was swarming with medusa-shaped creatures (jellyfish) averaging about six inches in diameter. As I stood pondering what a painful death it would be were one to fall into the water among those venomous creatures, I suddenly realized that their movements were identical to that of the huge thing that I saw rise up from and return to the depths off Bermuda. Could we have seen a monstrous jellyfish? Who can really say what creatures the sea shelters, for the average depth of the ocean is sixteen thousand feet, and in some areas the surface and bottom are separated by thirty-five thousand feet of water.

Although the sighting of the strange creature that came up out of the depths and Verity's being attacked by lightning were occurrences that might well be explained scientifically, one must admit that they were not incidents one would normally encounter. They could be called highly unusual. But what about incidents that defy scientific explanations?

Thirty-two-year-old John Fairfax became the first man to row across the Atlantic alone. In 1969, it took the Englishman six months to row his twenty-foot boat, the *Britannia*, from the Canary Islands to Fort Lauderdale. He rowed right through the "Devil's Triangle."

During a press conference upon his arrival, he was asked what was the most exciting thing about his journey. He paused momentarily. He then began to tell of two "flying saucers" that threatened to cut short his voyage. "One night at about 20 degrees above the horizon I saw two bright lights. They were ten times as bright as Venus. They weren't stars. The two objects climbed into the sky and then separated. One flying low and the other flying high. The high one mounted toward the constellation of Ursa Major.

Then the two disappeared. While the two bodies were visible," Fairfax said, "a strange feeling came over me similar to a hypnotic trance. It was a funny feeling like someone was asking me to go away. I kept telling it 'no.'" After the objects disappeared, the trance passed, and Fairfax discovered that the cigarette he'd been holding was nothing but a long gray ash, and he had broken into a violent sweat.

If you are ever in Fort Lauderdale and visit one of the larger yacht basins, chances are that you'll see a character who looks like he stepped from the pages of "Terry and the Pirates." He is six feet three of walking muscle. More distinguished than his height is his flaming red hair and a beard to match. The tattoos covering his arms tell of his many years in the navy. The people who step out of his way as he saunters down the dock tell of his ruggedness. From his tan uniform and cap, one knows that John Carpenter is a charter boat captain. When rower John Fairfax completed his voyage across the Atlantic, John Carpenter greeted him on his arrival in Florida. However, when Fairfax told of his encounter with the two UFOs, Carpenter scoffed at the story as a publicity hoax. For over a year John Carpenter referred to Fairfax's story as a wild tale of the sea. But no longer does the rugged captain mock. In fact, he doesn't scoff at any UFO stories anymore.

One summer night the red-bearded seafarer was returning from Bimini aboard his charter boat. The passengers and mate were sleeping below. The moon was full and the sea flat calm. Carpenter was looking ahead trying to pick up the glow from the lights of Fort Lauderdale. It was shortly after midnight. Something was different, but at first he paid little notice. Then he realized that the foredeck, which should have been reflecting the white light of the moon's glow, was casting a greenish reflection. "I leaned out of the cabin window and looked up. I couldn't believe what I saw. Directly above the boat were two greenish glowing disk-shaped objects . . . just hovering there. I was completely awestruck. I watched the two objects for . . . I don't know how long. I was about to call the others on deck when the two objects plunged into the sea without hardly any splash. I watched their glow disappear far down into the depths." John Carpenter, who no longer scoffs at UFO reports, went on, "I didn't report the incident when I reached Fort Lauderdale because people tend to ridicule you when you tell them that you've experienced something that might be supernatural."

M. B. Dykshoorn of Miami is a parapsychological consultant who has lectured before university groups, been instrumental in the solution of several murders in Europe, and whose predictions have been better than 65 percent accurate. In other words, Dykshoorn is a successful clairvoyant. He has opinions about the mystery of the "Devil's Triangle." "There is nothing mysterious about half the disappearances that take place in the 'Devil's Triangle.' They are the result of natural causes. Of the remaining, some may be considered supernatural in that we are not familiar with the type of incident that may have caused them to vanish, but I visualize a scientific reason. When I have this vision, the breath is sucked from my lungs. I have trouble breathing," he said. The psychic gasped and continued, "I see aviators suffocating because all of the air is pulled from their lungs. They can't breathe. Even with oxygen and pressurized cabins they are suffocating . . . it is a giant vortex or whirlpool that originates from a hole in the floor of the ocean . . . maybe caused by the cooling of the earth's interior. When it reaches the surface, it pulls in all of the surrounding air. It can pull in airplanes flying as high as ten thousand feet. It pulls down big ships and anything that floats leaving no trace." He took in a deep breath and said, "In the near future an airliner with eighty to ninety people will go down out there and not leave a trace behind."

Shortly after Dykshoorn's statement, I had to take a trip to Puerto Rico. Although my personal feelings about the "triangle" lean toward the agnostic side, the first thing that I did when I boarded the plane in Miami was to count the number of passengers to be sure that there weren't "eighty to ninety people" aboard. There were seventy-nine including the crew and myself. I stayed on the plane. Since then, whenever I am about to embark on a flight over some part of the "triangle," I find myself counting the number of people aboard the plane.

Eight thousand persons in distress is a lot of people in trouble. But that is how many calls the Seventh District Coast Guard, headquartered in Miami, makes each year. The Seventh District, whose jurisdiction takes in most of the "Devil's Triangle," handles more distress calls and participates in more search and rescue operations than any other similar organization in the world. As you read this, there is indubitably a ship, boat, or aircraft from the Seventh District participating on a sea search. The odds are that the coast guardsmen will find whomever they are seeking, for their record is outstanding. But on the other hand, what if the subject of their search has already succumbed to the vexation of the "Devil's Triangle"? What does the United States Coast Guard think about this area? Coast guard journalist Ron Wright prepared the following release as the official opinion of the Seventh District commander.

Mysterious, mystic, supernatural . . . unlikely! This area, commonly bounded by Bermuda, Florida, and Puerto Rico might have on the surface what would be considered a high disappearance rate, but you also have to consider the amount of air and sea traffic in this area. Thousands of ships, small boats, and commercial and private aircraft transit the waters off Florida's east coast. The majority of disappearances in this area can be attributed to its unique environmental features; first the Gulf Stream, with its turbulence and swiftness, can quickly erase any sign of disaster; and second, the weather in the Caribbean-Atlantic area, with its ability to change rapidly, can produce thunderstorms and waterspouts without warning, making pilots and navigators face sudden catastrophe.

The topography of the ocean floor in the area between San Juan and Bermuda varies from extensive shoal areas in the islands to some of the deepest trenches in the world. With the interaction of strong currents over many reefs, the topography is constantly changing and hazards to the mariner can be swift.

There are some possible justifications for frequent accidents and so-called mysterious disappearances within the area, but the Coast Guard is not impressed with explanations from the supernatural. The combined unpredictable forces of man and nature are sufficient enough to supply unexplainable occurrences.

A problem we face here in south Florida is the large number of boaters transiting the waters between Florida's Gold Coast and the Bahama Islands. Too many times, people will attempt to make the crossing with a boat too small, a lack of knowledge of the area, and a lack of good seamanship, but they insist on trying. That's what keeps Coast Guard Air Station Miami the busiest search and rescue facility in the world. When people exercise less than mature judgement, show no respect for the sea, and venture into it, the odds are against them.

The Coast Guard feels there is nothing mysterious about

disappearances in the particular section of this ocean. Weather conditions, equipment failure, and human error, rather than something from the supernatural, are what have caused these tragedies.

In 1969, the Grumman Aircraft Company in cooperation with the navy and NASA undertook an oceanographic project known as the *Gulf Stream Drift Mission*. The expedition centered around a research submarine, the *Ben Franklin*, which was under the command of Jacques Piccard. This submersible vehicle drifted from off Palm Beach almost to New England utilizing the push of the Gulf Stream and other ocean currents. After the mission was completed, the crew of six reported seeing many things that were unusual, but nothing unexplainable. Probably the biggest mystery was the lack of sea life observed as the sub hovered between three hundred feet and twenty-two hundred feet.

Having done the underwater exterior motion picture filming of the *Ben Franklin*, I was given an opportunity to take a voyage in the vehicle. We descended to a depth of twelve hundred feet off Freeport in the Bahama Islands. It was amazing how rapidly the light diminished after three hundred feet. At five hundred there wasn't even a glow when one looked up at the surface. It was total darkness. As we touched bottom at twelve hundred feet, the sub's lights were turned on. The ocean floor was like a desert. A shrimp swimming in and out of a beer can and a small unidentifiable shark were the most interesting things that I observed on my voyage to the bottom of the "Devil's Triangle."

But again, does this mean that there is nothing mysterious going on out there? Who knows? I still adhere to the theory "Show me, and I'll believe you." Yet, when I was working as a photographer at Cape

Canaveral in 1962, a navy Polaris missile was launched and sent on its way down range into the Caribbean. A number of witnesses reported seeing a UFO alongside the missile. Reportedly, it was even picked up on radar. The Air Force attributed the sighting to a weather balloon sent aloft shortly before the launch.

However, a week later, a notice was posted on the bulletin board of the Range Photography Building at the cape to the effect that should any of the photographers observe strange or out-of-the-ordinary objects while tracking missiles with their cameras, they were to concentrate their photography on the UFO. None were filmed, nor were any more sighted.

One of the most asked questions concerning the "Devil's Triangle" seems to be, Why are the number of disappearances in the area so prevalent compared to other areas? The United States Coast Guard attributes it, among other things, to the large amount of sea and air traffic in that part of the ocean. Scientists refer to the large number of meteorological and oceanographic anomalies that occur in the area.

On the supernatural side, the disciples of the late Edgar Cayce adhere to the philosophy that the lost city of Atlantis is located well within the confines of the "Devil's Triangle." In fact, Cayce pinpointed the sunken metropolis as having been near the present island of Bimini some fifty miles east of Miami. The Cayceites ascribe to the cause of the mysterious losses of ships and planes as being a powerful energy source far down in the depths of the ocean emanating destructive forces at certain unpredictable intervals. UFOologists have not pushed their theories of UFOs being responsible for the disappearances even though certain magazines and writers have exploited that hypothesis. However, dedicated UFO researchers report that there are dozens and dozens of other areas on the face of the earth where UFO sightings are far more prevalent than in the "Devil's Triangle," and there are no strange kidnappings or disappearances in those other areas.

The southern capes, Cape Horn and the Cape of Good Hope, have been responsible for more missing vessels than the "triangle." But in those sections of the southern oceans violent storms are a major cause as is well-known by mariners who have voyaged through those seas.

Yet there exists another area where mysterious disappearances of ships, planes, and yachts occur even more often than in the "Devil's Triangle." If one were to bore almost straight through the center of the earth from a point near the center of the "Devil's Triangle," he would come out in an area off the east coast of Japan—an area referred to as the "Devil's Sea."

The "Devil's Sea," which is actually triangular in shape, is bounded by the southeast coast of Japan, the northern tip of the Philippines, and Guam. It covers a far greater expanse than the "Devil's Triangle," which probably accounts for the higher incidence of disappearances there. In fact, during the years following World War II, the Japanese government became concerned enough over the number of unexplained losses that it sent a large research vessel on an exploration mission to see what was happening. The research vessel apparently did find out what was going on out there—for it was never seen or heard from again.

There exists between the "Devil's Triangle" and the "Devil's Sea" another similarity other than disappearing ships and planes. It is a parallelism that, although coincidental, is more than circumstantial. If you have even a basic knowledge of navigation or studied physics in high school, you will remember that the compass does not point to the true North Pole but rather to the magnetic North Pole. This is called compass variation. At different locales around the earth the amount of variation differs. In some places, it can be more than 20 degrees, which means the navigator must compensate for this and add or subtract 20 degrees when determining his compass heading. However, there are two longitudinal or meridian areas where compass variation does not exist. In other words, in these two places the compass points to the true north rather than the magnetic north. One of these places is off the east coast of Florida. The other is off the east coast of Japan. So both the western extremity of the "Devil's Triangle" and the western extremity of the "Devil's Sea" are the only two meridians where the compass actually points to the true north. As one moves east from these longitudes, the compass variation increases with equal proportionality.

Could magnetism or some form of magnetic phenomenon be related to the strange disappearances in the two areas in question? Soon after the five TBM Avengers disappeared in 1945, the United States Navy conducted a five-year study called Project Magnet. After the study was completed, its results remained classified for many years. Finally, when the results were released, they gave no indication of anything strange or unusual in the area of the study, which took place within the area we refer to as the "Devil's Triangle." Some individuals have accused the government of holding back certain results of the study. However, there is no proof one way or the other. But there was a strange occurrence that could be related to the matter of magnetic phenomena. In the chapter titled "To Beyond the Wild Blue Yonder," you read about the huge navy P5M patrol bomber that took off from Hamilton, Bermuda, on the night of November 9, 1956, and was never seen again. The plane was a modified Mariner flying boat and carried a crew of ten. Its mission was classified. The craft was equipped with a magnetic anomaly detector. This device is not to be confused with a magnetometer used to detect steel hulls of submerged submarines. It is an instrument with which to study magnetic flux density or abnormal magnetic phenomena.

There have been many incidences of compass needles spinning wildly for no apparent reason on vessels or aircraft passing through the "triangle." Some yachtsmen have had complete electrical systems burn out and their compasses rendered useless. They made it to port only because their boats were diesel powered and depended on compression rather than electric ignition to operate. Others have journeyed through the "triangle" dozens or even hundreds of times without seeing or experiencing anything unusual. But then, think back about all of those who entered the "triangle" for the first time and never emerged from it.

Whether it is natural or supernatural will be a topic of conversation from the waterfront bars of Kowloon to the casinos of the Caribbean for many years to come. It is just like the numerous UFO sightings reported in the southeastern United States in September, 1973. Not only did private citizens make reports, but so did numerous police officers and military personnel. In fact, two military policemen on duty at Hunter Air Force Base, Georgia, reported that their patrol vehicle was forced off the road by a UFO. Police in five different Alabama cities reported sightings in one night. All reported the crafts as having green-and-white lights. The Georgia State Police reported that a glowing green cylinder found in a field near Manchester was nothing more than a signal flare. The sighting at Hunter AFB, which is south of Savannah, is the nearest to the "triangle" that any of the objects were sighted. In spite of the numerous sightings, there were no mysterious disappearances. An air force report attributed the sightings to "space junk" reentering the earth's field of gravity. Whether "space junk" or strange visitors, there was absolutely nothing to associate the sightings with the "Devil's Triangle."

Human error, mechanical malfunction, structural failure, weather phenomena, the supernatural, or whatever else might be causing ships, planes, and yachts to vanish in the "Devil's Triangle" will continue to occur. It is quite possible that at this very minute some unfortunate aviator or mariner is out there fighting for his life as he discovers one of the secrets of the "Devil's Triangle."

Bibliography

Brown, Slater, *The World of the Wind*. New York: The Bobbs-Merrill Co., Inc., 1961.

Chapman, Charles, *Piloting, Seamanship, and Small Boat Handling*. Motor Boating, Inc., 1960.

Cooney, David, *A Chronology of the United States Navy, 1775–1965*. New York: Franklin Watts, Inc., 1965.

Gaddis, Vincent H., *Invisible Horizons: True Mysteries of the Sea*. Pennsylvania: Chilton Book Company, 1965.

Godwin, John, *This Baffling World*. New York: Hart Publishing Co., 1972.

Hoehling, A. A., *They Sailed Into Oblivion*. Thomas Yoseloff Co., 1958.

Potter, E. B., "The Prisoners of the *Cyclops*," in *The Naval Academy Magazine*. U. S. Navy publication.

Potter, John, Jr., *The Treasure Diver's Guide*. New York: Doubleday and Company, Inc., 1960.

Riggs, J. L., *Bahama Islands*. D. Van Nostrand Company, Inc., 1949.

Slocum, Joshua, *Sailing Alone Around the World*. New York: Dover Publications, Inc., 1956.

Smith, S. E., editor, *The United States Navy in World War II*. New York: Ballantine Books.

Tomalin, Nicholas and Ron Hall, *The Strange Last Voyage of Donald Crowhurst*. New York: Stein and Day, 1970.

Vihlen, Hugo, *April Fool: Or How I Sailed from*

Casablanca to Florida in a Six Foot Boat. Illinois: Follett Publishing Company, 1971.

"Bermuda Triangle Bibliography," Thesis by Larry Kusche, University of Arizona, 1973.

"Blue Jackets' Manual," U.S. Navy publication, 1914.

"Naval Aviation News," June, 1973.

"Principal Marine Disasters, 1831-1932," U.S. Coast Guard publication.

"Stories of Strange Sights As Retold from St. Nicholas," *St. Nicholas Magazine.* Century Co., 1922.

Index

217

ABOUT THE AUTHOR

RICHARD WINER was born in Sioux Falls, South Dakota, and attended the University of Minnesota, graduating with a degree in education in 1951. He served in the U.S. Navy during World War II, seeing action in the Pacific. A documentary filmmaker, Mr. Winer recently made a film, narrated by Vincent Price, with the same title as this book, THE DEVIL'S TRIANGLE. Richard Winer researched THE DEVIL'S TRIANGLE for four years prior to its publication, sailing in his own sailboat, the forty-five foot *Running Bowline*, to all the perimeters of the region, flying over the area by airplane and even visiting the sea floor, twelve hundred feet beneath it. Mr. Winer's hobbies, besides sailing, include collecting prewar vintage sports cars. His many classic cars include: a 1933 Alfa-Romeo two-seater, a 1934 SS Jaguar, a 1930 Invicta and a 1935 Ford Coupé, plus a number of prewar trucks. At present, Mr. Winer is writing his second book, entitled *Cyclops,* an in-depth study of one of the many ships to disappear in the "Devil's Triangle."

LISTEN!!

We represent world-famous authors (many published by Bantam), newsmakers, personalities and entertainers who know how to grab and hold an audience's attention and at the same time, make them enjoy listening. And their fees fit many budgets.

So if you, or someone you know, sets up discussions, debates, forums, symposiums or lectures you should get in touch with us.

We're the BANTAM LECTURE BUREAU and we'll send you a free copy of our catalog which will tell you exactly who we represent and what they talk about.

OTHER WORLDS.
OTHER REALITIES.

In fact and fiction, these extraordinary books bring the fascinating world of the supernatural down to earth from ancient astronauts and black magic to witchcraft voodoo and mysticism—these books look at other worlds and examine other realities.

- ☐ THE DEVIL'S TRIANGLE (8445/$1.50)—Fact
- ☐ POWER THROUGH WITCHCRAFT (8673/$1.25)—Fact
- ☐ CHARIOTS OF THE GODS (Q5753/$1.25)—Fact
- ☐ A COMPLETE GUIDE TO THE TAROT (Q6696/$1.25)—Fact
- ☐ WITCHCRAFT AND BLACK MAGIC (7996/$1.95)—Fact
- ☐ THE EXORCIST (X7200/$1.75)—Fiction
- ☐ GODS FROM OUTER SPACE (Q7276/$1.25)—Fact
- ☐ NOT OF THIS WORLD (7696/$1.25)—Fact
- ☐ GOD DRIVES A FLYING SAUCER (7733/$1.25)—Fact
- ☐ THE SPACESHIPS OF EZEKIEL (8378/$1.95)—Fact

Bantam Book Catalog

It lists over a thousand money-saving best-sellers originally priced from $3.75 to $15.00 —bestsellers that are yours now for as little as 50¢ to $2.95!

The catalog gives you a great opportunity to build your own private library at huge savings!

So don't delay any longer—send us your name and address and 10¢ (to help defray postage and handling costs).